Workshop & Study Guide

The Practical Guide to Contracts & Other Essential Knowledge

Dr. Dondi M. Day

Workshop & Study Guide for The Practical Guide to Contracts & Other Essential Knowledge

ISBN: 979-8-3302-9050-5 (paperback)

Published by Emerald Isle Publishing, Inc.
PO Box 5041
Emerald Isle, NC 28594

dondi.day@emeraldislepublishing.com

Legal Disclaimer

THE INFORMATION PROVIDED IN THIS STUDY GUIDEBOOK IS DESIGNED TO ENHANCE YOUR UNDERSTANDING OF CONTRACT PRINCIPLES BUT SHOULD NOT BE CONSTRUED AS LEGAL ADVICE. ALWAYS CONSULT WITH AN ATTORNEY FOR SPECIFIC LEGAL QUESTIONS OR CONCERNS

The information provided in this study guide is intended for educational purposes only and should not be considered a substitute for professional legal counsel. The author expressly disclaims any liability arising from the use or reliance on the information contained herein. Before entering into any contractual agreement, terminating a contract, or pursuing any legal action, it is strongly advised to consult with a qualified attorney. This guide does not provide an exhaustive overview of all contract types or specific contract forms available in the marketplace. Instead, it aims to provide a general understanding of common contract terms and conditions, their potential risks, and strategies for managing claims and disputes. The clauses presented in this guide are examples of provisions often found in contracts, illustrating both benign and problematic scenarios. This guidebook does not constitute legal advice and should not be interpreted as such. Contract law is constantly evolving, so it's important to understand changes in legislation, regulations, or industry standards. For advice regarding specific problems or circumstances, please consult with a legal professional.

Table of Contents

Introduction

In the complex landscape of project execution, contracts are the bedrock upon which successful endeavors are built. They serve as the guiding framework, outlining the roles, responsibilities, and expectations of all parties involved. A comprehensive understanding of the contract's structure, terms, and conditions is not merely beneficial but essential for both project managers and executives to steer projects toward triumph, mitigate potential pitfalls, and foster enduring, mutually beneficial business relationships.

For Project Managers

- Clear Roadmap: Contracts provide a detailed blueprint for project execution. Project managers well-versed in contract intricacies can effectively strategize, allocate resources, and manage timelines, ensuring alignment with the agreed-upon terms.
- Risk Mitigation: Contracts frequently include provisions addressing risk allocation, change management, and dispute resolution. A nuanced understanding of these clauses empowers project managers to proactively identify and mitigate potential risks.
- Stakeholder Management: Contracts delineate the roles and responsibilities of various stakeholders. Project managers fluent in contract language can effectively communicate expectations, navigate conflicts, and facilitate seamless collaboration among all parties.
- Performance Tracking: Contracts often stipulate specific performance metrics and milestones. Project managers with a firm grasp of these requirements can accurately monitor progress, detect deviations, and implement corrective actions promptly.
- Financial Command: Contracts detail payment terms, invoicing procedures, and financial obligations. Project managers familiar with these intricacies can adeptly manage project finances, ensuring punctual payments and adherence to budgetary constraints.

For Executives

- Strategic Decision-Making: Contracts serve as a compass for executive decision-making regarding project investments, resource allocation, and risk tolerance. A profound understanding of contract terms equips executives to accurately assess potential risks and rewards, guiding them towards optimal choices.
- Legal Compliance: Contracts are legally binding instruments. Executives must prioritize adherence to contractual obligations to safeguard their organization from legal disputes, financial penalties, and reputational harm.
- Relationship Cultivation: Contracts lay the groundwork for long-term business relationships. Executives who grasp the subtleties of contracts can foster positive rapport with clients, partners, and suppliers, fostering repeat business and collaborative opportunities.
- Financial Stewardship: Contracts carry significant financial implications. Executives must comprehend the financial provisions within contracts to ensure profitability, manage cash flow effectively, and protect the organization's financial health.

- Reputation Management: An organization's reputation hinges on its ability to fulfill its contractual commitments. Executives who champion contract comprehension can uphold and elevate their organization's reputation for reliability and professionalism.

Conclusion

A comprehensive grasp of contract structure, terms, and conditions is not a luxury but a necessity for both project managers and executives. This knowledge empowers them to navigate the complexities inherent in projects, adeptly manage risks, make informed decisions, cultivate robust relationships, and diligently safeguard their organization's interests. This mutual understanding fosters a collaborative environment that consistently meets expectations, executes projects with excellence, and fosters enduring business relationships. This mutual understanding fosters a collaborative environment that consistently meets expectations, executes projects with excellence, and fosters enduring business relationships.

Module Overviews

Module 1: Fundamentals of Contract Language and Risk Reduction: This module equips you with the knowledge to confidently interpret and navigate contracts. It covers contract fundamentals, terminology, and interpretation principles, empowering you to protect your interests and ensure project success.

Module 2: Mastering Notices, Waivers, and Change Orders: This module delves into essential communication tools that safeguard your interests, prevent disputes, and ensure smooth project execution. You'll learn how to draft effective notices, understand the implications of waivers, and manage change orders to minimize disputes.

Module 3: Documentation Best Practices for Claims Prevention and Defense: This module focuses on proactive project documentation management. It covers the types of documents to create and maintain, document control systems, documenting project events, managing Requests for Information (RFIs), and drafting persuasive claim letters.

Module 4: Navigating Subcontractor Claims and Disputes: This module equips you with the skills to effectively handle subcontractor claims and disputes. It covers understanding subcontractor agreements, managing subcontractor performance, resolving disputes, and protecting against potential claims.

Module 5: Effective Communication and Relationship Management for Subcontract and Procurement Success: This module emphasizes the importance of building strong relationships and effective communication in construction projects. It covers strategies for building relationships, holding effective meetings, defining roles and responsibilities, fostering open communication, and resolving issues promptly.

Module 6: Preparing, Drafting, and Defending Claims: This module delves into the complexities of construction industry claims. It covers preparing for claims, drafting effective claim documents, responding to and defending against claims, and providing case studies and practical exercises to reinforce your understanding.

Notes:

Module 1: Fundamentals of Contract Language and Risk Reduction

This module is designed to equip project managers and executives with the knowledge and tools to confidently interpret and navigate contracts. It covers contract fundamentals, terminology, and interpretation principles, empowering project managers to protect their interests and ensure project success. It is broken down into four parts:

Part One: Setting the Foundation. This section provides a basic overview of contracts, including the different types of contracts, the elements of contract formation, and how to choose the right contract type for a project. It also covers some basic legal concepts, such as offer, acceptance, consideration, and legality of purpose.

Part Two: Interpretation. This section discusses how courts interpret contracts when there is a disagreement. It covers the plain meaning rule, contextual interpretation, the parol evidence rule, contra proferentem, and other principles of contract interpretation. It also discusses some common pitfalls in contract interpretation, such as ambiguity, inconsistency, and omissions.

Part Three: Understanding Contract Structure. This section explains the typical structure of a contract, including the preamble, recitals, definitions, body, and schedules or exhibits. It also discusses the importance of using clear and concise language in contracts.

Part Four: Exploring Contract Terms and Conditions. This section provides an overview of some of the most common contract terms and conditions, such as acceptance of products and services, audit clauses, assignment clauses, change clauses, compliance with laws and regulations clauses, confidentiality clauses, and many more. It also discusses the risks associated with each clause and provides advice on how to mitigate them.

Part One: Setting the Foundation

1. What is a Contract?

A contract is a legally binding agreement between two or more parties. It's like a promise that can be taken to court if someone doesn't keep their word. Each party promises to do something (or not do something) in exchange for something else of value.

Notes:

___

___

___

___

2. What Does a Contract Do?

A contract is a tool to manage risk. It allows one party to transfer risks to the other party, providing some protection.

___

___

___

___

Types of Contracts

Contracts are the foundation of projects across different industries. Different contract types are designed to address specific needs and risks. Here are the main types:

- Fixed-Price Contracts: The price is set up front and doesn't change, even if the project costs more than expected. This is good for predictable budgets but riskier for the contractor.
- Cost-Reimbursable Contracts: The contractor is paid for all project costs, plus an extra fee. This is flexible but can be riskier for the buyer if costs go over budget.
- T&M Contracts: The contractor is paid for the time spent and materials used. This is flexible for projects with an uncertain scope, but it can result in higher costs.

Choosing the Right Contract Type

- Project Scope: Well-defined scope favors fixed-price contracts; uncertain or evolving scope leans towards cost-reimbursable or T&M.
- Risk Allocation: Determine which party is best positioned to manage and absorb risk.

- Budget Constraints: Fixed-price offers budget certainty, while cost-reimbursable and T&M can accommodate changing financial requirements.
- Project Duration and Complexity: Long-term, complex projects might benefit from the flexibility of cost-reimbursable or T&M contracts.

Elements of Contract Formation

The elements of a contract consist of the offer (i.e., intent), acceptance, and consideration.

- Offer: A proposal made by one party to another, indicating a willingness to enter into a contract under specified terms.
- Intent refers to the parties' determination to act or perform in a particular manner. It's essentially the will or purpose behind the promises made in the agreement.
- Acceptance: The other party's agreement to the offer's terms. Acceptance must be unconditional and communicated to the offeror.
- Consideration: The value that each party brings to a contract is considered. It's the essential reason why the parties are entering into the agreement. In a contract, the owner's consideration is typically the promise to pay the contractor for their work, while the contractor's consideration is the promise to perform the work according to the specified terms and conditions.

Notes:

____

____

____

____

3. How Do You Know When a Contract is Complete?

A contract is complete when you have fulfilled all your contractual obligations outlined in it.

Notes:

____

____

____

____

4. What is the Definition of Term and Condition?

A term refers to any provision that (1) addresses a specific topic and (2) obligates one or both parties. A condition is a contingency that either activates (e.g., condition precedent) or suspends (i.e., condition subsequent) a specific term.

Notes:

____

____

____

____

5. What is Legality of Purpose?

For a contract to be enforceable, the work or services performed cannot involve illegal activities.

Notes:

____

____

____

____

6. Who are the Parties to a Contract?

There are typically at least two parties to a contract. All persons and organizations that have not signed the contract are considered third parties and do not have a direct contractual relationship called privity of contract.

Notes:

____

____

____

____

7. What are Competent Parties?

To have an enforceable contract, all parties must be competent and have the legal and mental capacity to form one.

Notes:

8. What are Conditional Acceptance and Counteroffers?

If your subcontractor gives you an offer with added strings attached, the response is considered a counteroffer, not an acceptance.

Notes:

9. What is Acceptance by Actions?

Acceptance isn't always communicated by words but by actions. For example, if you offer to buy a product at a specific price, and the seller responds by shipping the goods, the seller's actions indicate acceptance of the offer.

Notes:

10. What are the Types of Authority?

Express authority and implied authority.

- Express Authority: This is the authority that is directly granted to an individual, either verbally or in writing. In a contract, this could be the project manager's authority to sign change orders up to a certain dollar amount, as explicitly stated in the contract.
- Implied Authority: This is the authority that is not expressly granted but is assumed to be necessary for an individual to carry out their duties. For example, a project manager might have the implied authority to order materials needed for the project, even if this is not

explicitly stated in the contract. This authority is inferred from the nature of their roles and responsibilities.

Notes:

____

____

____

____

11. What is Privity of Contract?

Privity of contract is merely the connection or relationship between two or more contracting parties. For instance, imagine a project where the owner (Party A) hires a general contractor (Party B) to build a new office building. The general contractor then hires a subcontractor (Party C) to install the plumbing. If the plumbing work is faulty and causes damage, the owner can sue the general contractor for breach of contract because they have privity of contract. However, the owner cannot directly sue the subcontractor because there is no direct contractual relationship between them; they lack privity. This means the owner's recourse is limited to suing the party they have a contract with, who is then responsible for addressing the issue with the subcontractor.

Notes:

____

____

____

____

Part Two: Interpretation

Before we move on, let's understand how courts interpret contracts if there's a disagreement.

Interpretation Key Points

Here are some key principles:

- Plain Meaning Rule: Courts look at the usual meaning of the words in the contract. If the language is clear, they'll enforce it as written.
- Contextual Interpretation: If the contract isn't clear, courts look at the situation when the contract was made, like what the parties discussed and what's common in the industry.
- Parol Evidence Rule: This rule says that if the contract is clear and complete, the court won't consider anything outside of the written contract to interpret it.
- Contra Proferentem: If a part of the contract is unclear, the court might interpret it against the person who wrote it. This encourages clear writing.
- Specific over General: If there's a conflict, specific parts of the contract are more important than general ones.
- Handwritten over Typed: Handwritten parts might be more important than typed ones if there's a conflict, as they show the parties' latest intentions.

Interpretation Pitfalls

Common pitfalls in contract interpretation include:

- Ambiguity: Vague or unclear language can lead to misunderstandings and disputes.
- Inconsistency: Conflicting provisions within the contract can create confusion and uncertainty.
- Omissions: Failing to address important issues can lead to disputes and unintended consequences.
- Overly Broad or Narrow Language: Using language that is too broad or too narrow can lead to unintended interpretations.
- Failure to Define Terms: Not defining key terms can lead to disagreements over their meaning.

To avoid these pitfalls, it is crucial that contracts are drafted with clear, concise, and unambiguous language. Define key terms, ensure consistency throughout the document, and address all relevant issues. If ambiguities arise, seek clarification from the other party!

Part Three: Understanding Contract Structure

Understanding how a contract is structured is akin to having a roadmap for a complex journey. It provides clarity and organization, making it easier to navigate the document's intricate details. Each section of a contract serves a specific purpose. The preamble identifies the parties and the agreement's start date, while the recitals offer crucial context and background information. Definitions clarify key terms, ensuring everyone is on the same page. The main body, the heart of the contract, lays out the rights, obligations, and dispute resolution mechanisms. Schedules or exhibits may be attached to provide detailed information. Headings and subheadings create a clear hierarchy, facilitating easy reference. Understanding this structure allows parties to interpret the contract accurately, enforce its provisions effectively, and ultimately achieve successful project outcomes.

Understanding The Outline And Structure Of Contracts

1. **How are contracts structured?** (see example at the end of this section) Contracts usually have these parts (though not always in this order):
    - Preamble: This is like the introduction. It identifies the contract, the parties, and the date.
    - Recitals: This explains the background or history of the agreement.
    - Definitions: This section defines important terms used in the contract.
    - Body: This is the main part of the contract with the key terms and conditions.
    - Schedules or Exhibits: These are extra documents attached to the contract with more details.

Notes:

____

____

____

____

2. **What is a preamble?**

The preamble is like the contract's ID card. It tells you the agreement's title, who the parties are, and the date it was made. It's important to get the parties' full legal names and where they're incorporated (if it's a company) right in this section.

Notes:

____

____

3. What are contract recitals?

This contract section describes or introduces the nature, background, or history of the contractual relationship between the parties.

Notes:

4. Are contract recitals part of the contract and admissible in court?

Recitals usually aren't considered part of the main contract terms, but a court might look at them to understand the contract's purpose or what the parties intended. If there's a conflict between the recitals and the main terms, the main terms win. But you can add a special clause to make the recitals a formal part of the contract.

Notes:

5. Is it possible to make the recitals part of the contract and admissible?

Yes, it is possible to make recitals part of the contract and potentially admissible in court. While recitals are traditionally considered introductory and non-binding, including a specific clause within the contract can change their legal status.

Notes:

6. **Risk Mitigation Strategy:**

To achieve this, insert the following clause into a new section titled "Incorporation of Recitals" within the body of the contract: "The recitals set forth above are an integral part of this Agreement and are incorporated herein by reference."

Explanation:

This clause explicitly states that the recitals are not merely prefatory but are considered essential components of the contract itself. By doing so, the parties elevate the status of the recitals, making them potentially admissible as evidence in court during a dispute. This can be crucial in clarifying the parties' intentions and understanding when the contract was formed, especially if ambiguities arise in the operative provisions of the contract.

Notes:

Additional Considerations:

While this clause strengthens the evidentiary value of recitals, their admissibility in court is still subject to the rules of evidence and the specific circumstances of the case.

7. What is an interpretation clause?

An interpretation clause sets out the rules of construction (i.e., the process of interpreting a law or a legal document) that the parties intend to apply to the contract.

Notes:

8. **What are definitions?**

The definitions section is essential for a clear, well-written contract, as well as a tool you have at your disposal to ensure consistency.

Notes:

---

9. What is the main body of a contract?

The body of the contract has the key terms governing the rights and obligations of the parties.

Notes:

---

10. What are headings?

Headings provide guidance and assistance in navigating the contract.

Notes:

EXAMPLE

MASTER SERVICES AGREEMENT

Preamble

This Master Agreement for Construction Services and Associated Construction Procurement and Management ("Agreement"), dated as of [insert date] (the "Effective Date"), is entered between ______________________________ ("Contractor") with a principal office located at ______________________________ and ______________________, a ______________________ corporation as ("Subcontractor") with its principal office located at ______________________. Contractor and Subcontractor are sometimes collectively referred to herein as "Parties" or individually as a "Party."

Recitals

WHEREAS, this Agreement is a written understanding between Contractor and Subcontractor containing contract clauses applying to future subcontracts (hereafter "Subcontracts") for the furnishing of construction and construction-related services, which may include, but not be limited to, design services,

WHEREAS, this Agreement contemplates separate future Subcontracts that will incorporate by reference and attach the requirements, applicable clauses, and documents agreed to herein and incorporated by reference.

NOW, THEREFORE, in consideration of the mutual covenants and agreements herein contained and other good and valuable consideration, the parties hereby agree as follows:

Main Body

Headings & Subheadings

ARTICLE 1

DEFINITIONS

1.1 Definitions.

Capitalized terms used without other definition shall have the meanings specified in this Section 1.1 or as defined within the body of the Agreement, unless the context requires otherwise.

"Applicable Insurance Policies" means all policies of insurance procured or obtained by Subcontractor in respect of the Project or the performance of the Work.

1.2 Construction and Intent of Documents

Unless otherwise provided, all references to "Articles," "Sections," and "Exhibits" are to Articles and Sections of, and Exhibits to, this Agreement. Wherever the words "include," "includes," or "including" are used in this Agreement, they shall be deemed to be followed by the words "without limitation." All references to "herein," "hereof," "hereunder," and similar terms shall be deemed to refer to this entire Agreement. References to any gender include all others if applicable in the

Part Four: Exploring Contract Terms and Conditions

A comprehensive grasp of contractual terms and conditions is paramount for all parties involved in a project. These terms delineate the rights, responsibilities, and expectations of each party, serving as a roadmap for project execution and risk allocation. Understanding these terms empowers project managers to effectively plan, mitigate risks, and manage stakeholders, while executives can make informed decisions, ensure legal compliance, and foster strong business relationships. Ultimately, a thorough understanding of contractual terms and conditions is essential for successful project outcomes, minimizing disputes, and promoting a collaborative and productive project environment.

Terms and Conditions

1. **What is the acceptance of products and services?**

Acceptance occurs when your customer (after having a reasonable opportunity to inspect the products or services) signifies that the goods and/or services conform to the contract or that they will take or retain them despite their non-conformity.

Risks: Imagine you're hiring someone to paint your house. If you don't clearly agree on what 'finished' looks like, you might end up arguing over whether the job is done right. That's why it's important to clearly define acceptance criteria in contracts.

Notes:

____

____

____

____

2. **What is an audit clause?**

This clause outlines your customer's right to require you to open your books for an audit periodically.

Risks: The risk of having to disclose sensitive financial information to the owner, potentially revealing proprietary pricing strategies or profit margins.

Notes:

____

____

____

____

3. What is an assignment clause?

Assigning means handing off the benefits and obligations of a contract from one party to another. An assignment clause may limit your right to assign your rights and responsibilities to another third party or require your customer's consent before an assignment can occur.

Risks: The risk of having the contract assigned to another party (i.e., competitor) without their consent, potentially leading to difficulties in performance or payment.

Notes:

____

____

____

____

4. What is a changes clause?

Most contracts include a changes clause that gives your customer flexibility to make reasonable (or within the general scope of the contract) changes to the scope.

Risks: The possibility of being required to perform additional work or changes without proper compensation or time extensions, resulting in cost overruns and delays.

Notes:

____

____

____

____

5. What is a compliance with laws and regulations clause?

Most contracts have compliance requirements that may expose your company to penalties, fines, reputation damages, and material loss if not evaluated and monitored.

Risks: The risk of non-compliance leading to legal penalties, fines, or project delays.

Notes:

____

____

6. **What is a confidentiality clause?**

A mutual confidentiality clause should protect both parties' confidential information from unauthorized disclosure.

Risks: The risk of inadvertently disclosing confidential information, leading to legal action or damage to business relationships.

Notes:

7. **What are contract documents?**

Risks: This clause outlines the list of documents that comprise the entire definition of "contract documents."

The contract frequently consists of various documents that, when combined, form its basis.

Notes:

8. **What are contractor responsibilities?**

This clause outlines your duties, obligations, and general responsibilities.

Notes:

9. **What is a coordination with others clause?**

This clause requires you to assume the responsibility for scheduling and coordinating your work with other subcontractors, vendors, and suppliers with whom you may not have a contractual relationship.

Risks: The risk of being held responsible for delays or disruptions caused by other parties on the project, even if they are not under the contractor's control.

Notes:

10. **What is a default clause?**

The default clause's purpose is to describe what happens in the event of a breach.

Risks: The risk of termination or other penalties for failing to meet contractual obligations, even if the failure is due to circumstances beyond the contractor's control.

Notes:

11. **What is a differing site conditions clause?**

A differing site condition is an unknown, latent, hidden, or concealed physical condition at the project site that is materially different from the conditions you anticipated or physical conditions indicated in the project's plans, specifications, and geotechnical reports.

Risks: The risk of encountering unexpected site conditions that increase the cost or time required for the project without adequate compensation or time extensions.

Notes:

___

___

___

___

12. What is a delays clause?

Project delays are a universal phenomenon and an unpleasant fact! Several reasons, including severe weather, differing site conditions, equipment problems, construction errors, or interference, can cause significant delays, and they are almost always accompanied by cost and time overruns. Is this clause in addition to a liquidated damages clause?

Risks: The risk of being held liable for delays, even if they are caused by factors beyond the contractor's control, such as weather events or owner-caused delays.

Notes:

___

___

___

___

13. What are delivery milestones?

Milestones are a series of gates you must pass through to continue your journey in construction.

Risks: The risk of not receiving payment for completed work if a milestone is not met, even if the delay is not the contractor's fault.

Notes:

___

___

___

___

14. What is a dispute resolution clause?

Dispute resolution clauses help parties avoid the expense and hassle of going to court and offer peace of mind that disputes will be resolved quickly and amicably.

Risks: The risk of being forced into a dispute resolution process that is not favorable to the contractor, such as arbitration in a distant location.

Notes:

____

____

____

____

15. What is an entire agreement clause?

This clause ensures that only the contract's four corners govern the parties' intentions and obligations.

Risks: The risk of being unable to rely on pre-contractual representations or agreements that are not explicitly included in the written contract.

Notes:

____

____

____

____

16. What is an error or inconsistency in the contract document clause?

This clause is crucial to include in your contracts. It requires the contracting parties to notify each other if they find an error or inconsistency in the contract and contract documents.

Risks: The risk of being held responsible for errors or inconsistencies in the contract documents, even if they were not caused by the contractor.

Notes:

____

____

17. What is an expediting clause?

Expediting language is often found within various contract clauses, or it may be a stand-alone clause to ensure the delivery of equipment and materials or work performance.

Risks: The risk of incurring additional costs to expedite work without being compensated for those costs, especially if the delay is not the contractor's fault.

Notes:

18. What are flow-down (or flow-through) and incorporated by reference clauses?

These clauses transfer significant risk to unwary subcontractors. A flow-down clause is often found in construction contracts, but its inclusion in other contracts, such as supply and engineering subcontracts, is becoming more common. An incorporation by reference clause is broader than a flow-down clause and tries to make all rights and obligations between the higher-tier parties apply.

Risks Specific to Subcontractors: The risk of being bound by the terms of the prime contract, even if those terms were not negotiated or agreed upon by the subcontractor.

Notes:

19. What is a force majeure clause?

Force Majeure contract clauses are standard and normally accepted. The aftermath of recent large-scale disasters, such as Hurricane Sandy, impacted 24 states. It flooded streets, tunnels, and subway lines and cut power to most major cities along the east coast of the United States for an extended period of time. If disaster strikes, whether from major hurricanes, floods, snowstorms, earthquakes, or epidemics, will your organization be liable for damages resulting from failure to meet the delivery or project's schedule?

Risks: The risk of not being excused from performance or not receiving adequate time extensions for delays caused by events beyond the contractor's control.

Notes:

____

____

____

____

20. What are governing laws (or choice of law) and venue clauses?

The governing law or choice of law clause allows the parties to agree that a specific state's laws will be used to interpret their agreement. A venue or jurisdiction clause often determines which state will have jurisdiction to litigate a case.

Risks: The risk of having to litigate disputes in a distant or inconvenient forum or under laws that are not favorable to the contractor.

Notes:

____

____

____

____

21. What are headings?

Headings provide guidance and assistance in navigating the contract.

Notes:

____

____

____

____

22. What is an indemnification clause?

Indemnification clauses are important but can be risky. They can shift responsibility for damages or losses to you, even if you weren't at fault. It's crucial to understand these clauses to protect your business.

Risks Specific to Subcontractors: The risk of being held liable for damages or losses caused by the contractor or owner, even if the subcontractor is not at fault.

Notes:

____

____

____

____

23. What are the types of damages?

- Actual damages: Also known as compensatory damages, these are intended to reimburse the injured party for specific, quantifiable financial losses suffered due to a breach of contract or other harmful act.
  - Examples: Medical bills, lost wages, property repair costs.
- General damages: These compensate for non-monetary losses that are difficult to quantify, such as pain and suffering, emotional distress, or loss of consortium.
- Direct damages: Losses that flow directly and immediately from the harmful act or breach of contract.
  - Examples: The cost of repairing a damaged car after an accident.
- Indirect costs: Costs that arise as a consequence of the harmful act or breach, but not directly from it.
  - Example: Lost profits due to business interruption after a fire.
- Special damages: This is a type of compensatory damage that covers specific out-of-pocket expenses incurred as a result of the harmful act.
  - Examples: Medical bills, lost wages.
- Consequential damages: This is a type of compensatory damage that covers indirect losses that were foreseeable as a result of the harmful act.
  - Example: Lost profits due to a delayed shipment.
- Nominal damages: A small amount awarded to acknowledge a legal wrong even when no actual financial loss occurred.
  - Example: $1 awarded for a technical breach of contract.

- Substantial damages: Damages that are more than nominal but less than the full amount of actual damages, awarded when precise calculation is difficult.
- Punitive damages: Also known as exemplary damages, these are awarded to punish the wrongdoer for malicious or grossly negligent behavior and deter future misconduct.
- Liquidated damages: A predetermined amount agreed upon by the parties in a contract to be paid in the event of a specific breach.
- Unliquidated damages: Damages that are not specified in the contract and must be determined by a court based on the evidence presented.

Notes:.

____

____

____

____

24. Can you be held liable for the actions of others?

Yes, if you agree to it in a contract, you can be held responsible in the eyes of the court.

Notes:

____

____

____

____

25. What are the three forms of indemnification?

- **Broad Form Indemnification:**

This type of clause requires the indemnitor (the party providing the indemnity) to compensate the indemnitee (the party receiving the indemnity) for all losses, damages, or liabilities arising from the indemnitor's work or services, regardless of who was at fault. This means that even if the indemnitee was partially or entirely responsible for the loss, the indemnitor would still be liable.

Risks: Broad-form indemnification is considered the most favorable to the indemnitee but the riskiest for the indemnitor.

Example: Subcontractor shall indemnify, defend, and hold harmless Contractor and its officers, directors, employees, agents, and representatives from and against any and all claims, damages, losses, liabilities, expenses, and costs, including reasonable attorneys' fees, arising out of or resulting from the performance of the work under this Agreement, regardless of whether or not such claim, damage, loss, or liability is caused in part by a party indemnified hereunder.

- **Intermediate Form Indemnification:**

This type of clause requires the indemnitor to compensate the indemnitee for losses, damages, or liabilities caused in part by the indemnitor's actions, but not if the indemnitee is solely responsible.

Risks: It is less favorable to the indemnitee than a broad form, but less risky for the indemnitor.

Example: Subcontractor shall indemnify, defend, and hold harmless Contractor and its officers, directors, employees, agents, and representatives from and against any and all claims, damages, losses, liabilities, expenses, and costs, including reasonable attorneys' fees, arising out of or resulting from the performance of the work under this Agreement, but only to the extent caused in part by any negligent act or omission of Subcontractor, or anyone directly or indirectly employed by them or anyone for whose acts they may be liable.

- **Narrow Form Indemnification:**

Also known as limited form indemnity, this clause requires the indemnitor to compensate the indemnitee only for losses, damages, or liabilities caused solely by the indemnitor's negligence or fault.

Risks: This is the least favorable form for the indemnitee and the least risky for the indemnitor.

Example: Subcontractor shall indemnify, defend, and hold harmless Contractor and its officers, directors, employees, agents, and representatives from and against any and all claims, damages, losses, liabilities, expenses, and costs, including reasonable attorneys' fees, arising out of or resulting from the performance of the work under this Agreement, but only to the extent caused by the sole negligence or willful misconduct of Subcontractor, or anyone directly or indirectly employed by them or anyone for whose acts they may be liable.

Notes:

____

____

____

____

- **Preferable Language:**

Subcontractor shall indemnify, defend, and hold harmless Contractor and its officers, directors, employees, agents, and representatives from and against any and all **third** party claims, damages, losses, liabilities, expenses, and costs, including reasonable attorneys' fees, **caused by** subcontractor's performance of the work under this Agreement, but only to the extent **caused by the sole negligence** or willful misconduct of Subcontractor, or anyone directly employed by them or anyone for whose acts they may be liable. In no event shall the total liability of Subcontractor to Contractor under the indemnity exceed the amount of general liability insurance coverage required under this Agreement. **This indemnification obligation shall expire one (1) year after the date of final acceptance of the Work.**

26. What is a limitation of liability clause?

The limitation of liability clause is another heavily negotiated and crucial clause you want to include in your contracts

Risks: The risk of the clause being unenforceable or not adequately protecting the contractor/subcontractor from certain types of damages.

Notes:

____

____

____

____

27. What are liquidated damages?

Liquidated damages are a predetermined amount of money that the parties agree will be paid as damages for a specific breach (e.g., delay in delivery). These are used when actual damages may be difficult to determine.

Risks: Having to pay excessive or unreasonable liquidated damages for delays, even if the actual damages are much lower.

Notes:

____

____

____

____

28. What is a no damages by contractor clause?

This clause aims to limit the contractor's liability for damages caused by events beyond their control, such as acts of God or delays caused by the owner.

Risks: The risk of not being able to recover damages from the owner for delays or disruptions caused by the owner or other parties.

Notes:

29. What is a no damages for delay clause?

This clause typically states that the contractor will not be entitled to any compensation for delays, even if they are caused by the owner or other parties. It is often used in construction contracts to protect the owner from cost overruns due to delays.

Risks: The risk of not being able to recover damages for delays, even if they are caused by the contractor, owner, or other parties.

Notes:

30. What is a notices clause?

A notices clause specifies how and where formal communications between the parties should be delivered (e.g., by certified mail, email, or personal delivery).

Risks: The risk of failing to provide timely or proper notice, which could result in the loss of rights or remedies under the contract.

Notes:

31. What is an order of precedence clause?

When multiple contract documents are involved, this clause establishes the hierarchy of those documents in case of conflicts or inconsistencies. For example, it might state that the special conditions take precedence over the general conditions.

Risks: There is a risk of ambiguity or conflict between different contract documents, leading to disputes over which document controls.

Notes:

---

32. What are pay-if-paid and pay-when-paid clauses?

Pay-if-paid clauses condition a subcontractor's payment on the contractor receiving payment from the owner. Pay-when-paid clauses delay payment to the subcontractor until a specified time after the contractor receives payment from the owner.

Risks Specific to Subcontractors: The risk of not receiving payment for completed work if the owner fails to pay the contractor.

Notes:

---

33. What is a price and payment clause?

This clause details the project's contract price, payment schedule, and any provisions for adjustments due to changes in the scope of work or other factors.

Risks: The risk of not receiving payment on time or in full or having to accept a lower price than agreed upon.

Notes:

---

34. What is a record retention clause?

This clause outlines how long each party must keep project-related records, such as invoices, correspondence, and inspection reports.

Risks: The risk of not being able to adequately defend against claims or disputes if records are not properly maintained.

Notes:

35. What is a scope of work clause?

The scope of work clause defines the specific tasks, deliverables, and responsibilities of each party involved in the contract.

Risks: There is a risk of scope creep or misunderstandings about the work to be performed, leading to disputes and additional costs.

Notes:

36. What is a set-off clause?

A set-off clause allows one party to deduct amounts owed to them by the other party from payments due under the contract.

Risks: The risk of having payments withheld or reduced due to unrelated claims or disputes.

Notes:

37. What is a severability clause?

If a court finds any provision of the contract to be invalid or unenforceable, a severability clause allows the rest of the contract to remain in effect.

Risks: The risk of having the entire contract invalidated if a single clause is found to be unenforceable, the entire contract may be invalidated.

Notes:

38. What is a survival clause?

This clause identifies which contract provisions continue to apply even after the contract has been terminated or completed.

Risks: The risk of having certain obligations continues to apply even after the contract has been terminated or completed.

Notes:

39. What are the special terms and conditions?

Special terms and conditions are project-specific provisions that are tailored to the unique requirements and circumstances of the contract.

Risks: There is a risk that these terms and conditions will be one-sided or unfavorable to the contractor.

Notes:

____

____

____

____

40. What is a suspension clause?

A suspension clause outlines the conditions under which one or both parties may temporarily suspend work on the project.

Risks: The risk of having work suspended without compensation or adequate notice, leading to financial losses and project delays.

Notes:

____

____

____

____

41. What is a term of contract clause?

This clause specifies the duration of the contract, including the start and end dates, and any provisions for extensions or early termination.

Risks: The risk of being locked into a long-term contract with unfavorable terms or being terminated early without cause.

Notes:

____

____

____

____

42. What is a termination for convenience clause?

This clause gives one or both parties the right to terminate the contract for any reason, without cause, by providing notice to the other party.

Risks: The risk of having the contract terminated without cause, potentially leaving the subcontractor and/or contractor without work or compensation for completed work.

Notes:

---

43. What is a time is of the essence clause?

This clause emphasizes that timely performance is critical to the contract, and failure to meet deadlines may be considered a material breach.

Risks: The risk of being held to strict deadlines, even if delays are caused by factors beyond the contractor's control.

Notes:

---

44. What is a title and risk of loss clause?

This clause addresses when ownership of the goods or materials passes from one party to another, and who bears the risk of loss or damage.

Risks: The risk of bearing the risk of loss or damage to goods or materials before they are delivered or accepted by the owner.

Notes:

---

45. What is a warranty clause?

A warranty clause guarantees the quality, performance, or condition of the goods or services provided under the contract.

Risks: The risk of being held liable for defects or malfunctions in the work or materials, even if they are not the subcontractor's and/or contractor's fault.

Notes:

____

____

____

____

46. What are waiver and release forms and contract language?

These are legal documents used to relinquish rights or claims. In a contractual context, they may be used to waive certain rights or release a party from liability for specific actions or events.

Risks: The risk of inadvertently waiving rights or releasing the owner from liability for certain actions or events.

Notes:

____

____

____

____

Notes:

Module 2: Mastering Notices, Waivers, and Change Orders

In the intricate dance of construction project management, effective communication is the rhythm that keeps everything in sync. Module 2: Mastering Notices, Waivers, and Change Orders delves into the essential communication tools that safeguard your interests, prevent disputes, and ensure smooth project execution. This module equips you with the knowledge and skills to navigate the complexities of notices, waivers, and change orders, empowering you to proactively manage risks and maintain positive relationships with all project stakeholders.

Part One: The Importance of Timely Notices. Timely notices are the unsung heroes of construction contracts. They serve as a formal communication mechanism, alerting parties to potential issues, delays, or changes that could impact the project. But their importance goes beyond mere communication; timely notices are often a contractual prerequisite for preserving your legal rights and remedies. This section delves into why timely notices are important, how to effectively leverage them, and the legal consequences of failing to comply with notice requirements. You'll gain a comprehensive understanding of the different types of notices, their specific purposes, and the critical role they play in protecting your interests throughout the project lifecycle.

Part Two: Drafting Effective Notices. Crafting clear, concise, and persuasive notices is both an art and a science. This section provides a step-by-step guide to drafting effective notices that comply with contractual requirements and clearly communicate your intentions. You'll learn about the essential elements of a well-crafted notice, including the importance of specific details, factual accuracy, and professional tone. Additionally, you'll explore how to tailor your notices to address various project scenarios, such as delays, change orders, claims, defaults, and terminations. By mastering the art of drafting effective notices, you'll be equipped to communicate your needs clearly, protect your rights, and avoid misunderstandings that could lead to costly disputes.

Part Three: Waivers and Their Implications. Waivers are powerful legal instruments that can significantly impact your rights and remedies in a construction project. This section demystifies waivers, explaining their purpose, potential risks, and best practices for their use. You'll learn about the different types of waivers, including conditional and unconditional waivers, and how they can be used to address issues like delays, defects, or non-compliance. You'll also explore the potential pitfalls of waivers, such as unintended scope, lack of consideration, or duress, and how to avoid them. Understanding the implications of waivers allows you to make informed decisions about when and how to use them to protect your interests.

Part Four: Managing Change Orders. Change orders are a fact of life in construction, but they don't have to be a source of conflict or confusion. This section provides a systematic approach to managing change orders, from evaluating their impact to negotiating and documenting the changes. You'll learn how to assess the scope, cost, and schedule implications of change orders, as well as how to communicate effectively with the owner and other stakeholders. By mastering the change order process, you can minimize disruptions, maintain project momentum, and ensure that changes are implemented smoothly and efficiently.

Part One: The Importance of Timely Notices: Safeguarding Your Interests in Construction Projects

Timely notices play a pivotal role in construction contracts, serving as a crucial communication tool between parties and a mechanism for protecting legal rights. Understanding the legal implications of notices and how to leverage them effectively is essential for successful project outcomes.

Why Timely Notices Matter

- Contractual Compliance: Most construction contracts contain specific notice provisions that outline the timing and content requirements for various notices, such as delays, change orders, or claims. Failure to provide timely notices as per the contract can result in a waiver of rights or remedies, even if the underlying claim is valid.
- Rights Preservation: Timely notices preserve the right to make claims or seek additional compensation for unforeseen events or changes that impact the project. They provide the other party with an opportunity to investigate the issue and potentially mitigate damages.
- Dispute Prevention: Promptly notifying the other party of potential issues can help prevent disputes from escalating by allowing for early resolution through negotiation or other alternative dispute resolution methods.
- Evidence and Documentation: Written notices create a clear record of events, issues, and claims, serving as valuable evidence in case of future disagreements or legal proceedings.

How to Leverage Notices to Protect Your Interests

- Know Your Contract: Thoroughly review your contract's notice provisions to understand the specific requirements for different types of notices. Pay attention to deadlines, required content, and delivery methods.
- Document Everything: Keep detailed records of all project-related events, including delays, changes, unexpected conditions, and any other issues that may affect the project. This documentation will be critical when creating notices.
- Act Promptly: Don't delay in sending notices when an issue arises. The sooner you notify the other party, the better your chances are of preserving your rights and avoiding disputes.
- Be Specific and Clear: Clearly state the nature of the issue, the relevant contractual provisions, the impact on the project, and the requested relief or action. Provide supporting documentation to substantiate your claims.
- Follow the Correct Procedure: Ensure that you follow the prescribed notice procedure outlined in the contract, including the correct form, content, and delivery method.
- Maintain Communication: After sending a notice, keep the lines of communication open with the other party. Be prepared to discuss the issue and explore potential solutions.

Legal Implications of Notices

- Failure to provide timely notices can have serious legal consequences. It can result in:

- Waiver of Rights: You may lose the right to make claims or seek compensation for an issue.
- Prejudice to the Other Party: The other party may argue that your failure to provide timely notice hindered their ability to investigate or mitigate the issue, resulting in increased damages.
- Dismissal of Claims: In litigation, a court may dismiss your claims if you failed to comply with the contract's notice requirements.

Part Two: Drafting Effective Notices

Notices are a critical communication tool in construction projects, serving as formal documentation of events, issues, or requests. Drafting effective notices is essential to protecting your rights, maintaining compliance with contractual obligations, and facilitating the timely resolution of disputes.

Key Elements of an Effective Notice

- Clear and Concise Language: Avoid jargon and technical terms. Use plain language that can be easily understood by all parties involved.
- Specific Details: Clearly identify the subject matter of the notice, including relevant dates, project references, and specific contractual provisions.
- Factual Accuracy: Ensure that all information presented in the notice is accurate and supported by evidence or documentation.
- Timeliness: Send the notice promptly after the event or issue arises, as delays can result in a waiver of rights or remedies.
- Professional Tone: Maintain a respectful and professional tone, even when addressing contentious issues.
- Proper Delivery: Follow the delivery method specified in the contract, whether it is certified mail, email, or personal delivery.

Addressing Various Project Scenarios

Delay Notice: Clearly state the cause of the delay, the anticipated impact on the project schedule, and any potential claims for additional time or compensation.

Notice of Change Order: Describe the proposed change in detail, including the scope of work, cost impact, and schedule implications.

Notice of Claim: Please specify the nature of the claim, the amount of damages sought, and the legal basis for the claim. Provide supporting documentation, such as invoices, photographs, or expert reports.

- Notice of Default: Identify the specific contractual provisions that have been breached and state the consequences of continued non-compliance. Provide the other party with an opportunity to cure the default within a reasonable timeframe.
- Notice of Termination: State clearly the reasons for termination, citing the relevant contractual provisions. Outline the parties' outstanding obligations or liabilities.

Additional Tips for Drafting Effective Notices

- Review Contractual Requirements: Thoroughly understand the notice provisions in your contract to ensure compliance with specific requirements.

- Seek Legal Counsel: If the issue is complex or involves significant financial or legal implications, consult with an attorney to ensure that the notice is properly drafted and protects your interests.
- Keep Copies: As part of your project documentation, maintain copies of all notices sent and received.

Study Questions:

1. **What is the importance of putting it in writing?**

Putting notices, disputes, and claims in writing is of paramount importance in the context of contracts and project management for several reasons:

- Evidence and Documentation: Written communication creates a clear and undeniable record of the issue, the parties involved, the date and time of the notice, and the specific details of the dispute or claim. This documentation is invaluable in the event of future disagreements or legal proceedings.
- Clarity and Precision: Written communication forces parties to articulate their positions clearly and precisely, reducing the risk of misunderstandings or misinterpretations that can arise from verbal discussions.
- Formalization: Written notices, disputes, and claims carry more weight and formality than verbal communication. They demonstrate a serious intent to resolve the issue and can prompt a more timely and effective response from the other party.
- Legal Compliance: Many contracts require written notice for certain events, such as delays, changes in scope, or disputes. Failure to provide written notice can result in a waiver of rights or remedies under the contract.
- Dispute Resolution: Written documentation is essential for resolving disputes through negotiation, mediation, arbitration, or litigation. It provides a basis for evaluating the merits of the claim and determining appropriate solutions.

Overall, putting notices, disputes, and claims in writing is a best practice that protects the interests of all parties involved, promotes transparency and accountability, and facilitates the efficient resolution of issues that may arise during a project.

Notes:

____

____

____

____

2. **How do you write an effective letter?**

To write an effective notice letter, you should:

- Be Clear and Concise: State the purpose of the letter upfront and avoid unnecessary jargon or technical terms.
- Be Specific: Clearly identify the issue or breach of contract, providing relevant dates, details, and supporting documentation.
- Be Professional: Maintain a courteous and professional tone, even if expressing dissatisfaction or disagreement.
- Be Timely: Send the notice letter promptly after the issue arises to avoid any potential waiver of rights or claims.
- Be Organized: Use a clear and logical structure, with headings and paragraphs, to make the letter easy to read and understand.
- Be Solution-Oriented: If applicable, propose a solution or course of action to resolve the issue amicably.
- Be Firm: Clearly state the consequences of non-compliance or failure to remedy the breach.

Notes:

____

____

____

____

3. What are the parts of a notice letter?

- Heading: Includes the sender's name, address, and contact information, as well as the recipient's name, address, and contact information. It also includes the date the letter was sent.
- Subject Line: A brief and clear statement summarizing the purpose of the letter (e.g., "Notice of Contract Breach," "Notice of Delay," "Notice of Claim").
- Salutation: A formal greeting addressing the recipient (e.g., "Dear Mr./Ms. [Recipient's Last Name]").
- Introduction: A concise statement of the purpose of the letter, referencing the relevant contract or agreement, and identifying the specific issue or breach.
- Body: Detailed explanation of the issue or breach, including relevant dates, facts, and supporting documentation. This section may also outline the contractual provisions that have been violated and the potential consequences of non-compliance.

- Demand or Request: A clear statement of what the sender expects the recipient to do to remedy the situation (e.g., cure the breach, provide compensation, take corrective action). This section may also include a deadline for the recipient's response.
- Conclusion: A brief summary of the sender's position and a reiteration of the demand or request. This section may also express a willingness to resolve the issue amicably and avoid further legal action.
- Closing: A formal closing (e.g., "Sincerely," "Yours faithfully") followed by the sender's signature and printed name.

Notes:

____

____

____

____

4. What are some communication skills that aren't taught but learned?

These learned skills include:

- Active Listening: Paying full attention to the speaker, asking clarifying questions, and summarizing what you've heard to ensure understanding.
- Empathy: Putting yourself in the other person's shoes to understand their perspective and feelings.
- Nonverbal Communication: Paying attention to body language, facial expressions, and tone of voice, both your own and the other person's.
- Conflict Resolution: Addressing disagreements or misunderstandings in a constructive and respectful manner.
- Negotiation: Finding mutually agreeable solutions to problems or disputes.
- Relationship Building: Establishing trust and rapport with others through open communication and collaboration.

These learned communication skills are essential for effective project management and contract administration, as they help to foster positive working relationships, prevent misunderstandings, and resolve conflicts in a timely and amicable manner.

Notes:

____

____

5. **What are some considerations about e-mail?**

- Professionalism: Maintain a professional tone and language in emails, as they may be used as evidence in legal disputes. Avoid using informal language, emojis, or excessive exclamation marks.
- Confidentiality: Be mindful of the sensitivity of information shared via email. Use appropriate confidentiality disclaimers and encryption if necessary.
- Retention: As part of your project documentation, keep copies of important project-related emails. This can be crucial in cases of disputes or audits.
- Organization: Use clear subject lines and organize emails in a logical manner to facilitate easy reference and retrieval.
- Timeliness: Respond to emails promptly and professionally, especially those related to project deadlines or critical issues.
- Attachments: Ensure that attachments are relevant, properly labeled, and in a format that can be easily opened by the recipient.
- Proofreading: Proofread emails carefully before sending to avoid errors or misunderstandings.

Notes:

6. **What are some other considerations about letters?**

- Format and Presentation: Use professional letterhead, proper formatting, and clear fonts to ensure readability and convey a sense of professionalism.
- Tone: Tailor the letter's tone to the specific situation and recipient. Be respectful and courteous, even when addressing disagreements or disputes.
- Confidentiality: If the letter contains sensitive or confidential information, clearly mark it as such and consider using secure delivery methods.

- Delivery Method: Depending on the urgency and importance of the letter, choose the appropriate delivery method. Options include certified mail, registered mail, courier services, or email (with delivery and read receipts).
- Record Keeping: Keep copies of all sent and received letters as part of your project documentation. This can be critical for both reference and potential legal purposes.

Notes:

____

____

____

____

Part Three: Waivers and Their Implications

Waivers are legal instruments where one party voluntarily relinquishes a known right or claim. While waivers can be useful tools for resolving disputes or streamlining project administration, they also carry potential risks and unintended consequences if not carefully crafted and understood.

What is a Waiver?

A waiver is essentially a voluntary and intentional abandonment of a legal right or claim. It can be expressed (clearly stated in writing or verbally) or implied (inferred from conduct). Waivers are often used in construction contracts to address issues like delays, defects, or non-compliance.

Potential Risks of Waivers

- Unintended Scope: Broadly worded waivers can inadvertently waive more rights than intended, leading to unforeseen consequences and potential losses.
- Lack of Consideration: For a waiver of rights to be enforceable, there must be consideration (something of value exchanged). If there's no consideration, the waiver may be deemed invalid.
- Duress or Coercion: Waivers obtained under duress or coercion (pressure or threats) are not enforceable. Both parties must voluntarily agree to the waiver.
- Ambiguity: Ambiguous language in a waiver can lead to disagreements over its interpretation and scope, potentially negating the waiver's intended purpose.
- Unconscionability: Courts may refuse to enforce waivers that are considered unconscionable (grossly unfair or one-sided).

Strategies to Avoid Unintended Waivers

- Clear and Specific Language: Ensure that the waiver clearly and specifically identifies the rights being waived, leaving no room for ambiguity or misinterpretation.
- Limited Scope: Avoid overly broad language that could encompass more rights than intended. The waiver should be tailored to the specific circumstances and issues at hand.
- Consideration: Ensure that there is valid consideration for the waiver, such as a monetary payment or a promise to perform certain actions.
- Voluntariness: Make certain that the waiver is executed voluntarily and without undue influence or coercion.
- Legal Review: Have an attorney review any waiver before signing to ensure it is legally sound and protects your interests.

Key Considerations for Waivers in Construction Contracts

- No-Damage-For-Delay Clauses: These clauses typically waive a contractor's right to claim damages for delays caused by the owner or other parties. Carefully consider the implications before agreeing to such a clause.
- Waiver of Consequential Damages: This clause limits the types of damages that can be recovered in the event of a contract breach. Ensure you understand the potential impact.

Waiver Language in Change Orders

- Waiver language in change orders refers to specific clauses or provisions that release or waive certain rights or claims related to the changes being made to the original contract.
- These clauses typically state that by signing the change order and accepting the agreed-upon compensation, the contractor waives any further claims for additional compensation or time extensions relating to that specific change.

Purpose of Waiver Language

- Finality and Certainty: Waiver language aims to provide finality and certainty to the change order process. It ensures that both parties agree on the scope of work, price, and schedule adjustments, preventing future disputes over these issucs.
- Risk Allocation: Waiver language helps allocate risks between the parties. By waiving certain claims, the contractor assumes the risk of any unforeseen costs or delays associated with the change, while the owner gains certainty regarding the final cost and schedule.
- Dispute Prevention: By clearly defining the scope of the change and the associated compensation, waiver language can help prevent costly and time-consuming disputes later on.

Common Types of Waiver Language in Change Orders

- General Release: This type of waiver broadly releases all claims related to the change order, including claims for additional compensation, time extensions, or impacts on other work.
- Specific Release: This type of waiver releases specific claims, such as claims for certain types of costs (e.g., labor, materials) or claims for delays caused by specific events.
- Reservation of Rights: While not technically a waiver, this clause allows the contractor to reserve the right to assert certain claims in the future, such as claims for unforeseen conditions or delays caused by the owner.
- Potential Risks and Considerations
- Overly Broad Language: Contractors should be cautious of overly broad waiver language that could inadvertently waive legitimate claims or rights.

- Unforeseen Circumstances: It's important to consider whether the waiver language adequately addresses unforeseen circumstances or events that may arise during the course of the changed work.
- Negotiation: Waiver language should be carefully negotiated between the parties to ensure it is fair and equitable.

Best Practices

- Review Carefully: Contractors should carefully review the waiver language in any change order before signing it.
- Seek Clarification: If any language is unclear or ambiguous, seek clarification from the owner or legal counsel.
- Negotiate: Don't be afraid to negotiate the terms of the waiver to ensure it adequately protects your interests.
- Documentation: Keep detailed records of all discussions and negotiations related to the change order and waiver language.

Waivers and Their Implications in Construction Liens

Lien waivers are specific types of waivers used in the construction industry to protect both the paying and receiving parties. They become particularly relevant when dealing with mechanics liens, which are legal claims placed on a property to secure payment for work performed or materials supplied.

Lien Waivers

Lien waivers are legal documents where a contractor, subcontractor, or supplier waives their right to file a mechanic's lien on a property in exchange for payment.

They serve as a receipt of payment and provide assurance to the paying party that they won't be subjected to a lien after making a payment.

Types of Lien Waivers

- Conditional Lien Waivers: These waivers are conditional upon the actual receipt of payment. If the payment is not received, the right to file a lien is not waived.
- Unconditional Lien Waivers: These waivers relinquish the right to file a lien, regardless of whether payment is received. They should only be signed after the payment has been confirmed.
- Partial Lien Waivers: These waivers release the right to file a lien for a specific amount or portion of work, allowing for progress payments.
- Final Lien Waivers: These waivers release all lien rights upon final payment for the entire project.

Importance of Lien Waivers

- Protection for Owners and Lenders: Lien waivers protect property owners and lenders from unexpected liens that could jeopardize their financial interests.
- Payment Assurance for Contractors and Suppliers: Lien waivers provide contractors and suppliers with written proof of payment, safeguarding their right to get paid for their work.
- Dispute Prevention: By clearly outlining the scope of work and payment terms, lien waivers can help prevent disputes over payment and lien rights.

Risks Associated with Lien Waivers

- Signing Too Early: Signing an unconditional waiver before receiving payment can leave contractors and suppliers vulnerable to non-payment.
- Inaccurate Information: If the lien waiver contains errors in the description of work, payment amount, or other details, it may not be enforceable.
- Overly broad language: Broadly worded waivers can unintentionally waive rights beyond the intended scope, potentially impacting future claims.

Best Practices for Lien Waivers

- Read Carefully: Thoroughly review the lien waiver before signing to ensure it accurately reflects the work performed and payment received.
- Conditional vs. Unconditional: Use conditional waivers until payment is received and confirmed.
- Accurate Information: Make sure that all information on the waiver is correct and matches the contract and payment details.
- Consult with Legal Counsel: If unsure about the terms or implications of a lien waiver, seek legal advice before signing.

Part Four: Managing Change Orders: A Systematic Approach to Minimizing Disputes in Construction Projects

Change orders are an inevitable part of most construction projects, often arising from unforeseen site conditions, design modifications, or client requests. Effective management of change orders is crucial for maintaining project timelines, budgets, and relationships between parties. Here's a systematic approach to evaluating, negotiating, and documenting change orders, ensuring transparency and minimizing the potential for disputes.

Establish a Clear Change Order Process

- Contractual Framework: Ensure your contract clearly defines the change order process, including who can initiate a change order, how it should be documented, the approval process, and the timeframe for decision-making.
- Standard Forms: Utilize standardized change order forms to ensure consistency and capture all relevant details, such as the scope of work, cost breakdown, schedule impact, and any waiver of claims language.
- Notification and Review: Create a clear communication channel for notifying the owner of potential changes, allowing sufficient time for review and approval before proceeding with the work.

Evaluate the Impact of the Change Order

- Scope Assessment: Thoroughly assess the scope of the proposed change and its impact on the project's overall timeline, budget, and resource allocation.
- Cost Analysis: Ask subcontractors and suppliers for detailed cost breakdowns for any additional labor, materials, or equipment required for the change.
- Schedule Impact: Evaluate the potential impact of the change on the project schedule, considering any delays or disruptions to critical path activities.
- Risk Assessment: Identify and assess any potential risks associated with the change order, such as safety concerns, unforeseen site conditions, or potential delays in obtaining permits or materials.

Negotiate and Document the Change Order

- Open Communication: Throughout the negotiation process, maintain open and transparent communication with the owner. Clearly explain the reasons for the change, the cost implications, and the schedule impact.
- Negotiation Strategies: Utilize effective negotiation techniques to reach a mutually agreeable solution. Consider factors such as the project's overall budget, the impact on the critical path, and the urgency of the change.
- Documentation: Ensure that all agreements and decisions are documented in writing using a formal change order document. Include detailed descriptions of the scope of work, pricing, schedule adjustments, and any waiver of claims language.

Implement and Monitor the Change Order

- Communication: Communicate the approved change order to all relevant parties, including subcontractors, suppliers, and project team members.
- Implementation: Ensure that the changed work is executed in accordance with the agreed-upon scope, schedule, and budget.
- Monitoring: Regularly monitor the progress of the changed work to identify any potential issues or deviations from the approved change order.

Review and Close Out the Change Order

- Verification: Verify that the changed work has been completed in accordance with the change order specifications and that all costs have been accurately documented.
- Final Documentation: Prepare a final change order document that summarizes the completed work, final costs, and any adjustments to the project schedule.
- Lessons Learned : Document any lessons learned from the change order process to improve future change management practices.

Module 3: Documentation Best Practices for Claims Prevention and Defense

In the dynamic world of construction, unforeseen events, changes, and disagreements are inevitable. These can lead to disputes and claims, which, if not managed effectively, can derail project timelines, strain budgets, and damage relationships. Module 3 equips you with the knowledge and skills to proactively manage project documentation, ensuring that you have the necessary evidence to prevent claims or defend your interests if disputes arise.

Part One: Project Documentation. This section emphasizes the critical role of comprehensive project documentation in claims prevention and defense. It explores the various types of documents that should be created and maintained throughout a project's lifecycle, from contracts and change orders to daily reports and meeting minutes. You'll learn how these documents serve as a valuable record of project activities, decisions, and communications, providing crucial evidence in case of disputes.

Part Two: Project Documentation Control. Effective document control is essential for managing the vast amount of information generated during a construction project. This section delves into the key elements of a robust document control system, including document identification, indexing, storage, retrieval, revision control, distribution, and archiving. You'll discover how implementing a well-organized system can streamline project workflows, enhance collaboration, and mitigate the risk of lost or misplaced information.

Part Three: Documenting Project Events. This section focuses on the importance of documenting key project events, such as meetings, site visits, inspections, delays, and changes. You'll learn how to create detailed and accurate records of these events, ensuring that you have the necessary evidence to support your position in case of disputes. Additionally, you'll explore best practices for documenting project events, including timeliness, accuracy, objectivity, and detail.

Part Four: Request for Information (RFI). RFIs are a common form of communication in construction projects, used to clarify ambiguities, seek additional information, or resolve discrepancies in contract documents. This section provides a comprehensive guide to managing RFIs effectively, from understanding their purpose and types to establishing a clear process for responding to them. You'll learn how to draft clear and concise RFI responses, track their status, and leverage them to prevent misunderstandings and potential claims.

Part Five: Drafting Persuasive Claim Letters. In the unfortunate event that a claim becomes necessary, crafting a persuasive claim letter is crucial for a successful resolution. This section provides a step-by-step guide to drafting effective claim letters, covering key elements such as clear language, factual accuracy, contractual basis, and quantification of damages. You'll also learn strategies for persuasive writing, anticipating counterarguments, and proposing solutions to facilitate a swift and amicable resolution.

Part One: Project Documentation

1. What is project documentation?

Project documentation is a collection of documents created throughout a project's life cycle. These documents serve as a comprehensive record of the project's planning, execution, and closure, outlining the project's goals, scope, budget, timeline, deliverables, risks, and communication strategies.

Project documentation serves several key purposes:

- Planning and Guidance: It helps the project team stay organized, focused, and aligned with the project's objectives by providing a clear roadmap for the project's execution.
- Communication and Collaboration: It facilitates communication among stakeholders, including team members, clients, and sponsors, by providing a shared understanding of the project's progress, challenges, and decisions.
- Decision-Making: It helps stakeholders make informed decisions based on accurate and up-to-date information about the project's performance and status.
- Risk Management: It identifies potential risks and outlines mitigation strategies to ensure the project stays on track and avoids costly delays or failures.
- Performance Evaluation: It allows for post-project evaluation, providing valuable insights and lessons learned that can be applied to future projects.
- Legal and Contractual Compliance: In many cases, project documentation is required to fulfill contractual obligations or demonstrate compliance with legal or regulatory requirements.

Examples of project documents include:

- Project Plan
- Scope Statement
- Pictures
- Video
- WBS
- Gantt Chart
- Budget
- Risk Register
- Meeting Minutes
- Status Reports
- Site Dairies

- Site Visitation Logs and/or Security Logs
- Spreadsheets
- Presentations
- Diagrams
- Lessons Learned Report

Notes:

____

____

____

____

2. **What are agendas?**

Agendas are essential for effective meetings. They provide a roadmap for the discussion, ensuring that all relevant topics are covered and that the meeting stays on track. Agendas also help participants prepare for the meeting, allowing them to gather any necessary information or materials beforehand.

Agendas can serve as evidence of:

- Notice: An agenda can prove that a party was aware of an upcoming discussion or decision.
- Intent: The topics listed on an agenda can shed light on the intentions of the parties involved in a meeting.
- Agreement: If decisions or agreements are recorded on an agenda, it could be used as evidence of those agreements.

Notes:

____

____

____

____

3. **What are the minutes of meetings?**

Meeting minutes are a written record of the discussions, decisions, and actions that took place during a meeting.

Meeting minutes can serve as evidence of:

- Notice: Minutes can prove that a party was aware of a discussion or decision.
- Intent: The minutes' contents can shed light on the intentions of the parties involved in a meeting.
- Agreement: If decisions or agreements are recorded in the minutes, they could be used as evidence of those agreements.

Notes:

4. **What are letters and other correspondence?**

- Transmittal Letters: These accompany other documents, providing context and a record of when and to whom they were sent.
- Confirmation Letters: These confirm verbal agreements or understandings reached during meetings or phone calls.
- Demand Letters: These formally request a party to fulfill a contractual obligation or remedy a breach.
- Notice of Default Letters: These inform a party that they have failed to meet a contractual obligation and may face consequences.
- Response Letters: These reply to previous correspondence, addressing concerns, providing clarifications, or proposing solutions.
- Letters of Intent: These express a non-binding intention to enter into a contract or agreement.
- Termination Letters: These formally end a contract, often stating the reasons for termination.
- Letters of Recommendation: These provide positive feedback about a contractor's or supplier's performance on a project.

These letters, along with meeting minutes, agendas, and other correspondence, contribute to a comprehensive record of project communications and decisions, which can be crucial in resolving disputes or demonstrating compliance with contractual obligations.

Notes:

5. **What are journals/project notebooks?**

Project journals, also known as project notebooks, are chronological records of daily activities, observations, and events that occur during a project. They serve as a detailed log of the project's progress, capturing information that may not be included in formal reports or other project documents.

Notes:

6. **What are daily site reports?**

Daily site reports provide detailed accounts of a construction site's day-to-day activities, progress, and observations.

Notes:

7. **What is a RACI matrix?**

A RACI matrix (also known as a Responsibility Assignment Matrix or RAM) is a project management tool used to define roles and responsibilities for each task, milestone, or decision within a project.

The acronym RACI stands for:

- Responsible: The person or group who does the work to complete the task.
- Accountable: The person who is ultimately answerable for the correct and thorough completion of the task and who delegates the work to those responsible.
- Consulted: The person or group who needs to be consulted before a decision or action is taken and who provides input or feedback.

- Informed: The person or group who needs to be kept up to date on the progress of the task but does not necessarily need to be consulted.

The RACI matrix is typically displayed as a grid, with tasks listed down the left side and team members or stakeholders across the top. Each cell in the matrix is assigned one of the RACI letters, indicating the person's role in that particular task.

Here are some of the benefits of using a RACI matrix:

- Clarifies roles and responsibilities: Helps to avoid confusion and duplication of effort.
- Improves communication and collaboration: Ensures everyone knows their role and who to communicate with.
- Facilitates decision-making: Identifies the key decision-makers for each task.
- Enhances accountability: Holds individuals accountable for their assigned tasks.

RACI matrices can be used in various types of projects and are particularly helpful in complex projects with multiple stakeholders. They can be created at the beginning of a project during the planning phase and updated as needed throughout the project's life cycle.

Notes:

____

____

____

____

Part Two: Project Documentation Control

Effective document control is essential for successful construction projects. With countless contracts, change orders, drawings, specifications, and correspondence, managing this volume of information can quickly become overwhelming. Implementing a practical document control system can help you stay organized, minimize risks, and ensure smooth project execution.

Why Document Control Matters

- Efficient Retrieval: Quickly locate and access specific documents when needed, saving time and resources.
- Version Control: Track revisions to ensure everyone is working with the latest version of documents, preventing costly errors and misunderstandings.
- Risk Mitigation: Protect against lost or misplaced information, reducing the risk of disputes, delays, and cost overruns.
- Enhanced Collaboration: Facilitate collaboration among project team members by providing a centralized repository for all project documentation.
- Compliance: Ensure compliance with contractual obligations, industry standards, and regulatory requirements.

Key Elements of a Document Control System

- Document Identification: Assign unique identifiers (e.g., numbers, codes) to each document to facilitate easy reference and tracking.
- Document Indexing: Create a comprehensive index or database of all project documents, including titles, dates, authors, and keywords for quick retrieval.
- Document Storage: Set up a secure and accessible storage system for both physical and electronic documents. Consider using cloud-based storage for easy access and collaboration.
- Document Retrieval: Implement a streamlined process for retrieving documents based on their identifiers, keywords, or other relevant criteria.
- Document Revision Control: Track revisions and changes to documents, ensuring that everyone has access to the latest versions. Consider using version control software to automate this process.
- Document Distribution: Establish clear procedures for distributing documents to relevant parties, ensuring that everyone has access to the information they need.
- Document Archiving: To maintain an organized system and avoid confusion, archive obsolete or superseded documents.

Implementing a Document Control System

- Assess Your Needs: Identify the types of documents you need to manage, the volume of information, and the specific requirements of your project.

- Choose the Right Tools: Select document control software or a combination of tools that best suit your needs and budget. Consider factors such as ease of use, scalability, and integration with other project management software.
- Define Roles and Responsibilities: Assign specific roles and responsibilities for document control, such as document controller, approvers, and reviewers.
- Establish Procedures: Develop clear and concise procedures for document creation, review, approval, distribution, revision, and archiving.
- Train Your Team: To ensure consistent and accurate use, train all project team members on the document control system and procedures.
- Monitor and Review: Regularly monitor the document control system's effectiveness and make adjustments as needed.

Part Three: Documenting Project Events

Thorough documentation of project events is essential for effective project management, dispute resolution, and legal compliance in the construction industry. By creating detailed records of meetings, site visits, inspections, and other relevant occurrences, you can ensure transparency, accountability, and informed decision-making throughout the project's life cycle.

1. **Why Document Project Events?**

- Evidence of Progress and Performance: Detailed records serve as proof of work completed, milestones achieved, and adherence to project schedules.
- Dispute Resolution: In cases of disagreements or claims, accurate documentation of events can be invaluable in supporting your position and resolving issues efficiently.
- Legal Compliance: Many contracts require documentation of specific events, such as inspections or change orders. Proper documentation ensures compliance and avoids potential legal complications.
- Risk Management: Identifying and documenting potential risks or issues early on allows for proactive mitigation and prevents them from escalating into costly problems.
- Communication and Collaboration: Well-documented events foster clear communication and collaboration among project stakeholders, ensuring everyone is informed and aligned.
- Lessons Learned: Documenting project events helps capture valuable lessons learned, which can be used to improve future projects and avoid repeating mistakes.

Types of Project Events to Document

- Meetings: Document key discussions, decisions, action items, and attendees of project meetings, including pre-construction meetings, progress meetings, and closeout meetings.
- Site Visits: Record observations, discussions, and any issues identified during site visits by project team members, inspectors, or other stakeholders.
- Inspections: Document the results of inspections conducted by building officials, quality control personnel, or other relevant parties. Include details on any deficiencies or non-compliance issues.
- Change Orders: Thoroughly document any changes to the project scope, schedule, or budget, including the reasons for the change, approvals, and associated costs.
- Delays and Disruptions: Record any events that cause delays or disruptions to the project, such as weather events, material shortages, or labor disputes.
- Safety incidents: Document any accidents, injuries, or near-misses on the job site, including the incident details, corrective actions taken, and lessons learned.

Best Practices for Documenting Project Events

- Timeliness: Document events as soon as possible, while the details are still fresh in your mind.
- Accuracy: Ensure that all information is accurate, complete, and unbiased.
- Objectivity: Avoid personal opinions or judgments. Stick to the facts and observations.
- Detail: Provide enough detail to capture the event's context and significance.
- Consistency: Use a consistent format and style for all documentation to ensure clarity and ease of reference.
- Storage: Maintain organized records of all project documentation in a secure and accessible location.

Part Four: Request for Information

Requests for Information (RFIs) are a common form of communication in construction projects, used to clarify details, resolve ambiguities, or gather additional information related to design, materials, or construction methods. Responding to RFIs promptly and accurately is crucial for maintaining project momentum, preventing delays, and fostering collaboration among project stakeholders.

Understanding RFIs

- Purpose: RFIs serve as a formal request for clarification or additional information from one party to another. They are typically initiated by contractors or subcontractors when they encounter unclear or conflicting information in the contract documents.
- Types: RFIs can cover a wide range of topics, including design details, material specifications, construction methods, code compliance, and project schedules.
- Importance: RFIs play a critical role in ensuring that everyone involved in the project has a shared understanding of the project requirements and expectations.

Strategies for Responding to RFIs

- Establish a Clear Process: Create a standardized process for handling RFIs, including assigning review responsibilities, establishing response timelines, and tracking the status of each RFI.
- Log and Track RFIs: Keep a detailed log of all RFIs received, including the date, requester, subject matter, and response deadline.
- Review Thoroughly: Carefully review each RFI to fully understand the question or request for information. If necessary, seek advice from relevant team members or experts.
- Respond Promptly: Aim to respond to RFIs within the agreed-upon timeframe or as soon as possible. Delays in responding can lead to project delays and disruptions.
- Provide Clear and Concise Answers: Respond clearly and concisely to the specific questions or requests raised in the RFI. Avoid vague or ambiguous responses.
- Include Supporting Documentation: If applicable, provide supporting documentation, such as drawings, specifications, or calculations, to substantiate your response.
- Collaborate: If the RFI raises a complex issue or requires input from multiple parties, collaborate with the relevant stakeholders to develop a comprehensive and accurate response.
- Document Responses: Keep track of all RFI responses and related correspondence. This documentation can be valuable in the event of future disputes or disagreements.

Benefits of Effective RFI Management

- Improved Communication: Promotes clear and transparent communication among project stakeholders.

- Reduced Risk of Errors: Clarifies ambiguities and inconsistencies in the contract documents, reducing the risk of costly errors or rework.
- Enhanced Collaboration: Fosters a collaborative approach to problem-solving and decision-making.
- Increased Efficiency: Streamlines the project workflow by addressing issues promptly and preventing unnecessary delays.
- Improved Project Outcomes: By facilitating clear communication and collaboration, effective RFI management contributes to successful project outcomes.

Additional Tips

- Prioritize RFIs: First, address RFIs that have the potential to impact the critical path or cause significant delays.
- Utilize Technology: Consider using RFI management software to streamline the process and track responses.
- Train Your Team: Ensure that all team members understand the RFI process and their roles and responsibilities.
- Learn from Past RFIs: Review past RFIs to identify recurring issues or areas where additional clarification may be needed.

Part Five: Drafting Persuasive Claim Letters

In the construction industry, claim letters are formal requests for additional compensation, time extensions, or other remedies due to unforeseen events, changes, or disputes that arise during a project. Crafting persuasive claim letters is crucial for maximizing your chances of a successful resolution and minimizing the need for costly and time-consuming litigation.

Key Elements of a Persuasive Claim Letter

- Clear and Concise Language: Avoid jargon and technical terms. Use plain language that can be easily understood by the recipient, who may not be familiar with construction-specific terminology.
- Strong Opening: Begin with a concise statement of the claim, clearly identifying the issue and the relief sought. This grabs the reader's attention and sets the tone for the rest of the letter.
- Factual Basis: Provide a detailed and factual account of the events or circumstances that led to the claim. Include relevant dates, project references, and any supporting documentation, such as contracts, change orders, photos, or expert reports.
- Contractual Basis: Clearly cite the specific contractual provisions that support your claim. This demonstrates that your claim is grounded in the legal agreement between the parties.
- Impact and Damages: Quantify the issue's impact on your project, including any delays, disruptions, or additional costs incurred. Provide a detailed breakdown of the damages sought with supporting documentation.
- Professional Tone: Maintain a professional and respectful tone throughout the letter, even if you are expressing frustration or disagreement. Avoid accusatory or inflammatory language.
- Call to Action: Conclude with a clear request for action from the recipient, such as a meeting to discuss the claim, a formal response by a specific deadline, or payment of the damages sought.

Strategies for Persuasive Writing

- Focus on Facts: Stick to the facts and avoid emotional or subjective language. Let the evidence and documentation speak for themselves.
- Highlight Strengths: Emphasize your claim's strengths, such as its clear contractual basis, the impact on the project, and the reasonableness of your requested relief.
- Anticipate Counterarguments: Consider potential counterarguments from the other party and address them proactively in your letter.
- Offer Solutions: If possible, propose potential solutions or compromises that could resolve the issue amicably.

- Maintain Credibility: Ensure that your letter is well-written, free of errors, and reflects a professional image.

Additional Tips for Claim Letters

- Timeliness: Submit your claim letter promptly after the issue arises to avoid any potential waiver of rights or claims.
- Legal Review: If the claim is complex or involves significant financial or legal implications, consult with an attorney to ensure that the letter is properly drafted and protects your interests.
- Documentation: Keep copies of all claim letters, responses, and related correspondence as part of your project documentation.

Notes:

Module 4: Navigating Subcontractor Claims and Disputes

Subcontractor claims and disputes are an unfortunate reality in the construction industry. They can stem from a variety of factors, such as delays, changes in scope, differing site conditions, payment issues, or disagreements over work quality. These disputes can lead to costly litigation, project delays, and strained relationships between parties. Module 4 equips you with the knowledge and skills to effectively navigate subcontractor claims and disputes, minimizing their negative impact on your projects.

Part One: Understanding Subcontractor Agreements. This section delves into the intricacies of subcontractor agreements, exploring the key provisions that govern the relationship between general contractors and subcontractors. You'll gain a comprehensive understanding of the terms and conditions that define each party's rights, responsibilities, and expectations. By understanding these provisions, you can proactively address potential issues, mitigate risks, and establish a solid foundation for a successful working relationship.

Part Two: Subcontractor Performance Management. Effective subcontractor management is crucial for ensuring that projects stay on track, within budget, and meet quality standards. This section provides practical strategies for monitoring and evaluating subcontractor performance, addressing performance issues promptly and constructively, and fostering a collaborative relationship built on trust and mutual respect. By implementing these strategies, you can minimize the likelihood of disputes and create a more productive and efficient project environment.

Part Three: Resolving Subcontractor Disputes. Despite the best efforts, disputes with subcontractors can still arise. This section explores various approaches to resolving these disputes, including negotiation, mediation, arbitration, and litigation. You'll learn about the advantages and disadvantages of each method, helping you choose the most appropriate approach for your specific situation. Additionally, you'll gain insights into how to prepare for and participate in dispute resolution processes effectively, maximizing your chances of a favorable outcome.

Part Four: Protecting Against Subcontractor Claims. Prevention is always better than cure. This section focuses on proactive strategies for minimizing the risk of subcontractor claims. You'll learn how to identify potential red flags, implement preventive measures, and establish clear communication channels to address concerns before they escalate into formal claims. By taking a proactive approach, you can protect your interests, avoid costly disputes, and maintain positive relationships with your subcontractors.

Part One: Understanding Subcontractor Agreements

Subcontractor agreements are critical documents that define the working relationship between general contractors and subcontractors on construction projects. These agreements outline the rights, responsibilities, and expectations of both parties, ensuring smooth and successful project execution. Understanding the key provisions of subcontractor agreements is essential for both parties to protect their interests and avoid potential disputes.

Key Provisions of Subcontractor Agreements

- Scope of Work: This section clearly defines the specific tasks, deliverables, and responsibilities of the subcontractor. It should include detailed descriptions of the work to be performed, the materials to be used, quality standards, and any applicable codes or regulations. A well-defined scope of work minimizes the risk of misunderstandings and disputes over the subcontractor's obligations.
- Payment Terms: This provision outlines the payment schedule, including the amount to be paid, the timing of payments (e.g., upon completion of milestones, monthly progress payments), and any retainage (a percentage of the payment withheld until the project is complete). It may also address payment for change orders or additional work. Clear payment terms are crucial for ensuring timely and accurate compensation for the subcontractor's work.
- Insurance Requirements: Subcontractor agreements typically require the subcontractor to carry certain types of insurance, such as general liability, workers' compensation, and automobile liability. The agreement should specify the minimum coverage limits and require the subcontractor to provide proof of insurance. Adequate insurance coverage protects both parties from potential liabilities and financial losses.
- Indemnification: Indemnification clauses allocate risk between the parties by requiring one party to compensate the other for losses or damages arising from specific events or circumstances. Subcontractor agreements often include indemnification provisions to protect the general contractor from claims or liabilities caused by the subcontractor's work.
- Termination: This provision outlines the conditions under which either party can terminate the agreement, such as non-performance, breach of contract, or insolvency. It may also specify the notice period required for termination, as well as any termination fees or penalties.
- Dispute Resolution: This clause establishes the process for resolving disputes between the parties, such as mediation, arbitration, or litigation. It may also specify the governing law and venue for any legal proceedings. A well-defined dispute resolution mechanism can help avoid costly and time-consuming litigation.

Additional Considerations

Flow-Down Provisions: These provisions incorporate the terms of the prime contract between the owner and the general contractor into the subcontractor agreement. This ensures that the subcontractor is bound by the same obligations and standards as the general contractor.

Change Orders: The agreement should address the process for handling change orders, including how they are initiated, approved, and priced.

Safety Requirements: The agreement may include specific safety requirements that the subcontractor must adhere to, such as compliance with OSHA regulations or project-specific safety plans.

Part Two: Managing Subcontractor Performance

Effective subcontractor management is crucial for the successful execution of construction projects. By proactively monitoring and addressing performance issues, general contractors can ensure that projects stay on schedule, within budget, and meet quality standards. Here are some strategies to effectively manage subcontractor performance:

Set Clear Expectations from the Start

- Detailed Scope of Work: Clearly define the subcontractor's scope of work in the contract, including specific tasks, deliverables, timelines, and quality standards.
- Communication Channels: Establish open and transparent communication channels with the subcontractor, outlining preferred methods of communication (e.g., email, phone, meetings) and frequency of updates.
- Performance Metrics: Define key performance indicators (KPIs) to measure the subcontractor's progress and performance, such as schedule adherence, quality of work, safety compliance, and responsiveness to communication.

Conduct Regular Performance Reviews

- Scheduled Meetings: Set up regular meetings with the subcontractor to review progress, discuss any issues or concerns, and provide feedback on their performance.
- Performance Reports: Request regular progress reports from the subcontractor, detailing work completed, upcoming tasks, and any potential challenges or delays.
- Site Inspections: Conduct regular site inspections to assess the quality of work, adherence to safety protocols, and overall progress.

Address Performance Issues Promptly

- Early Identification: Proactively identify potential performance issues through regular communication, performance reviews, and site inspections.
- Open Communication: Address any concerns or issues with the subcontractor in a timely and constructive manner. Clearly communicate your expectations and provide specific feedback on areas that need improvement.
- Corrective Action Plans: If performance issues persist, work with the subcontractor to develop a corrective action plan that outlines specific steps to be taken to address the issues and improve performance.
- Contractual Remedies: If the subcontractor fails to meet contractual obligations or address performance issues, consider invoking contractual remedies, such as termination, back charges, or liquidated damages.

Foster a Collaborative Relationship

- Open Communication: Encourage open and honest communication with the subcontractor, creating a collaborative environment where issues can be raised and addressed constructively.
- Mutual Respect: Treat the subcontractor with respect and professionalism, recognizing their expertise and contributions to the project.
- To Consider offering incentives for early completion, exceptional quality, or outstanding safety performance to motivate the subcontractor and reinforce positive behavior.

Document Everything

- Written Communication: Document all communication with the subcontractor, including emails, meeting minutes, phone calls, and site visit reports.
- Performance Records: Maintain detailed records of the subcontractor's performance, including progress reports, inspection results, and any corrective action plans.
- Change Orders: Document any changes to the scope of work or schedule through formal change orders.

Part Three: Resolving Subcontractor Disputes

Disputes are an unfortunate reality in the construction industry, and subcontractor conflicts are no exception. However, not every disagreement needs to escalate into a costly and time-consuming legal battle. Alternative Dispute Resolution (ADR) techniques offer effective ways to resolve disputes while maintaining relationships and minimizing disruptions to the project.

Understanding Alternative Dispute Resolution (ADR)

- ADR refers to various methods of resolving disputes outside of traditional litigation.
- It aims to provide faster, more cost-effective, and less adversarial solutions than going to court.
- ADR methods are often preferred in construction due to their flexibility and focus on preserving working relationships.

Types of ADR Techniques

Negotiation:

- This is the most informal and common ADR method.
- Involves direct discussions between the parties to reach a mutually agreeable solution.
- Can be facilitated by a neutral third party (facilitated negotiation).
- Advantages: Cost-effective, confidential, preserves relationships.
- Disadvantages: May not be successful if parties are unwilling to compromise or have significant power imbalances.

Mediation:

- Involves a neutral third party (mediator) who facilitates communication and helps parties reach a voluntary settlement.
- The mediator does not make decisions but helps parties identify common ground and explore options.
- Advantages: Confidential, which is less adversarial than litigation, can lead to creative solutions.
- Disadvantages: Requires the willingness of both parties to participate and compromise.

Arbitration:

- A more formal process where a neutral third party (arbitrator) hears both sides of the dispute and renders a binding decision.
- Similar to a court hearing but less formal and often faster.
- Advantages: Faster and less expensive than litigation, it can be binding or non-binding.
- Disadvantages: Limited right to appeal; less control over the process compared to negotiation or mediation.

Mini-Trial:

- A structured settlement process in which each side presents a case summary to a neutral advisor and senior executives of the disputing parties.
- The advisor provides a non-binding opinion on the likely outcome of the case if it went to trial.
- Advantages: It helps parties assess the strengths and weaknesses of their case and encourages settlement.
- Disadvantages: Can be expensive, may not be suitable for all types of disputes.

Dispute Review Boards (DRBs):

- A panel of neutral experts (usually three) hears disputes as they arise during the project.
- The DRB issues non-binding recommendations for resolving the dispute.
- Advantages: Provides timely resolution of disputes, can prevent issues from escalating.
- Disadvantages: May not be suitable for all types of disputes, can be expensive.

When to Escalate Disputes

- If initial attempts at negotiation or mediation fail, consider escalating to arbitration or another ADR method.
- If the dispute involves complex legal issues or high stakes, legal counsel may recommend litigation.
- Consider the contract's dispute resolution clause, which may mandate a specific ADR method or escalation process.

Choosing the Right ADR Technique

- The choice of ADR technique depends on a variety of factors, including the nature of the dispute, the relationship between the parties, the desired level of formality, and cost considerations.

Part Four: Protecting Against Subcontractor Claims

Subcontractor claims can be a major source of disruption, delays, and cost overruns in construction projects. By taking a proactive approach and implementing effective risk management strategies, general contractors can minimize the likelihood of claims and protect their interests.

Understanding Subcontractor Claims

- Common Causes: Subcontractor claims often arise from issues such as delays, changes in scope, differing site conditions, non-payment, or disputes over work quality.
- Impact: Claims can lead to costly litigation, project delays, strained relationships, and damage to reputation.
- Prevention: Proactive measures can significantly reduce claims risk and promote a more collaborative project environment.

Strategies for Minimizing Subcontractor Claims

Thorough Documentation:

- Clear Contracts: Ensure that the subcontract agreement clearly defines the scope of work, payment terms, schedule, and other key provisions.
- Change Orders: Document any changes to the scope of work or schedule through formal change orders, clearly outlining the revised terms and any associated costs or time adjustments.
- Daily Reports: Maintain detailed daily reports documenting work progress, weather conditions, site issues, and any other relevant events.
- Communication Records: Keep track of all communication with the subcontractor, including emails, meeting minutes, and phone calls.

Timely Communication:

- Regular Meetings: Schedule regular progress meetings with the subcontractor to discuss project status, address any concerns, and resolve issues before they escalate into claims.
- Prompt Responses: Respond to subcontractor inquiries and requests for information (RFIs) promptly and thoroughly.
- Open Communication: Foster open and transparent communication with the subcontractor, encouraging them to raise any concerns or issues early on.

Adherence to Contract Terms:

- Payment: In accordance with the contract terms, ensure timely and accurate payment to the subcontractor.
- Schedule: Maintain a realistic project schedule and communicate any changes or delays to the subcontractor promptly.

- Scope of Work: Avoid scope creep by clearly defining the subcontractor's responsibilities and obtaining written change orders for any additional work.
- Dispute Resolution: Follow the contractually agreed-upon dispute resolution process, such as mediation or arbitration, to resolve any disagreements in a timely and cost-effective manner.

Proactive Risk Management

- Risk Identification: Identify potential risks that could lead to subcontractor claims, such as design errors, unforeseen site conditions, or material shortages.
- Risk Mitigation: Develop and implement strategies to mitigate identified risks, such as conducting thorough site investigations, obtaining adequate insurance coverage, and maintaining contingency plans.
- Early Warning Signs: Monitor the subcontractor's performance for early warning signs of potential problems, such as missed deadlines, quality issues, or financial difficulties.

Fairness and Collaboration

- Fair Treatment: Treat the subcontractor fairly and respectfully, fostering a positive working relationship.
- Collaboration: Encourage collaboration and teamwork between the general contractor and subcontractor to achieve shared project goals.
- Incentives: Consider offering incentives for early completion, exceptional quality, or safety performance to motivate the subcontractor and promote a positive work environment.

Notes:

Module 5: Effective Communication and Relationship Management for Subcontract and Procurement Success

In the intricate landscape of construction projects, effective communication and relationship management are the linchpins that hold everything together. Module 5 delves into the strategies and practices that empower project managers and executives to foster strong, collaborative relationships with subcontractors, suppliers, and other key stakeholders. This module emphasizes that successful project outcomes are not solely determined by technical expertise but also by the ability to build trust, communicate openly, and navigate the complexities of human interactions.

Part One: Building Strong Relationships. This section explores the fundamental principles and strategies for cultivating strong relationships with subcontractors and suppliers. It emphasizes the importance of clear communication, mutual respect, fairness, transparency, collaboration, and a long-term perspective. By investing in these relationships, project managers and executives can create a positive and productive project environment, minimize the risk of disputes, and achieve superior project outcomes.

Part Two: Holding Effective Meetings. Meetings are essential for communication and collaboration on construction projects. This section provides a comprehensive guide to planning, conducting, and following up on effective meetings. It covers various types of meetings, including project kickoff meetings, biweekly and monthly project review meetings, and daily standup meetings. By mastering the art of holding effective meetings, project teams can streamline decision-making, resolve issues, and foster a sense of teamwork.

Part Three: Defining Roles and Responsibilities. Clearly defining roles and responsibilities is crucial for avoiding confusion, duplication of effort, and conflicts in construction projects. This section outlines the key steps involved in defining roles and responsibilities, including identifying key roles, developing a responsibility matrix, documenting roles and responsibilities, communicating clearly, and regularly reviewing and updating. By implementing these practices, project teams can ensure that everyone understands their role and contribution to the project, leading to improved accountability, communication, and collaboration.

Part Four: Open and Transparent Communication. Open and transparent communication is the lifeblood of successful construction projects. This section emphasizes the importance of fostering open communication channels, encouraging dialogue, practicing active listening, holding regular meetings, being transparent about project decisions and challenges, establishing feedback mechanisms, and addressing conflicts constructively. By prioritizing open communication, project teams can build trust, enhance collaboration, and proactively address issues before they escalate into major problems.

Part Five: Prompt Issue Resolution. In the dynamic world of construction, issues and conflicts are inevitable. This section focuses on the importance of addressing issues promptly and effectively to minimize disruptions, maintain project momentum, and preserve relationships. It provides strategies for early issue identification, open communication, collaborative problem-solving, timely decision-making, documentation, and escalation processes. By implementing these strategies, project teams can proactively manage risks, resolve conflicts amicably, and ensure project success.

Part One: Building Strong Relationships

In the construction industry, building strong relationships with subcontractors, suppliers, and other project stakeholders is essential for achieving project success. A collaborative and productive environment fosters trust, communication, and mutual respect, leading to smoother project execution, fewer disputes, and ultimately better outcomes for all parties involved.

Strategies for Building Strong Relationships

- Clear Communication: From the outset, establish open and transparent communication channels. Clearly communicate expectations, project goals, timelines, and any potential challenges. Encourage regular communication and feedback to promptly address concerns and prevent misunderstandings.
- Mutual Respect: Treat all stakeholders with respect and professionalism, recognizing their expertise and contributions to the project. Value their input and opinions, and create a collaborative environment where everyone feels heard and valued.
- Fairness and Transparency: Ensure fair treatment in all interactions, including contract negotiations, payment terms, and dispute resolution. Be transparent about project decisions, challenges, and changes, fostering trust and understanding among stakeholders.
- Collaboration and Teamwork: Encourage collaboration and teamwork among all project participants. Foster a sense of shared responsibility and ownership for project success. Celebrate achievements and milestones together, recognizing the contributions of each team member.
- Timely Payments: Pay subcontractors and suppliers on time, as per the agreed-upon terms. Prompt payment demonstrates respect for their work and helps build trust and goodwill.
- Flexibility and Adaptability: Be flexible and adaptable in your approach, recognizing that unforeseen challenges and changes are inevitable in construction projects. Work collaboratively with stakeholders to find solutions and adapt to changing circumstances.
- Conflict Resolution: Address conflicts or disagreements promptly and constructively. Utilize effective communication and problem-solving skills to find mutually agreeable solutions. Consider mediation or other alternative dispute resolution methods if necessary.
- Relationship Building: Invest time in building relationships beyond contractual obligations. Attend industry events, participate in networking opportunities, and engage in social activities to foster personal connections and strengthen professional relationships.

- Long-Term Perspective: Focus on building long-term relationships rather than short-term gains. A reputation for fairness, integrity, and collaboration will attract high-quality subcontractors and suppliers to future projects.

Benefits of Strong Relationships

- Improved Communication: Open communication channels lead to better understanding, fewer misunderstandings, and faster resolution of issues.
- Increased Efficiency: Collaboration and teamwork streamline project workflows, reduce delays, and improve overall project efficiency.
- Reduced Risk of Disputes: Trust and mutual respect minimize the likelihood of conflicts and disputes, saving time and resources.
- Enhanced Reputation: A reputation for fairness and collaboration attracts top talent and strengthens your position in the industry.
- Repeat Business: Building strong relationships with subcontractors and suppliers increases the likelihood of repeat business and referrals.

Part Two: Holding Effective Meetings

Meetings are a cornerstone of communication and collaboration in construction projects. When conducted effectively, meetings can streamline decision-making, resolve issues, and foster a sense of teamwork among project participants. However, poorly planned or executed meetings can be unproductive, time-consuming, and even detrimental to project progress. Here's a guide to holding effective meetings that drive project success:

Define the Purpose and Objectives

- Clear Purpose: Clearly define the meeting's purpose. Is it to share information, make decisions, brainstorm ideas, or resolve conflicts?
- Specific Objectives: Establish specific and measurable objectives for the meeting. What do you want to accomplish by the end of the meeting?
- Agenda: Create a detailed agenda that outlines the topics to be discussed, the time allotted for each topic, and the desired outcomes. Share the agenda with participants in advance to allow them to prepare.

Invite the Right Participants

- Essential Attendees: Invite only those individuals who are essential to the meeting's purpose and objectives. Avoid inviting people who are not directly involved or whose presence would not add value to the discussion.
- Roles and Responsibilities: Clearly define the roles and responsibilities of each participant, such as facilitator, note-taker, or decision-maker.

Manage the Meeting Effectively

- Start on Time: Begin the meeting promptly at the scheduled time, even if some participants are late. This shows respect for those who arrived on time and sets a professional tone.
- Follow the Agenda: Stick to the agenda as closely as possible, keeping discussions focused and on track.
- Encourage Participation: Create a safe and inclusive environment where all participants feel comfortable sharing their ideas and opinions.
- Manage Time: Keep track of time and ensure that each topic is given adequate attention without exceeding the allotted time.
- Summarize Key Points: Summarize key points and decisions throughout the meeting to ensure everyone is on the same page.
- Action Items: Assign clear action items to specific individuals with deadlines for completion.

Follow Up After the Meeting

- Meeting Minutes: Distribute meeting minutes promptly, summarizing key discussions, decisions, and action items.

- Follow-Up Actions: Ensure that assigned action items are completed within the agreed-upon timeframe.
- Feedback: Ask participants for feedback on the meeting's effectiveness and identify areas for improvement.

1. Additional Tips for Effective Meetings

- Prepare in Advance: Review the agenda and any relevant materials before the meeting.
- Be Respectful: Listen actively to others, avoid interrupting, and maintain a professional demeanor.
- Stay Focused: Avoid distractions and side conversations.
- Use Visual Aids: To enhance understanding and engagement, use visual aids, such as presentations or whiteboards.
- End on time: If all objectives have been met, conclude the meeting at the scheduled time or earlier.

The Importance of Project Kickoff Meetings

A project kickoff meeting is the formal launchpad for any project. It's more than introductions; it's about setting the tone, aligning expectations, and ensuring everyone understands the mission. A well-run kickoff meeting can significantly increase the likelihood of project success.

Key Objectives

- Shared Understanding: Ensure everyone involved has a clear picture of the project's goals, scope, and timeline.
- Team Building: Foster a sense of collaboration and excitement.
- Risk Mitigation: Identify potential roadblocks early on.
- Communication Setup: Establish communication channels and protocols.
- Buy-In: Get stakeholders excited and committed to the project.

Components of an Effective Kickoff Meeting

Preparation:

- Agenda: Create a detailed agenda with time allocations for each topic.
- Invitees: Carefully consider who needs to be present (core team, stakeholders, decision-makers).
- Materials: Prepare any necessary documents (project plan, timeline, budget overview).

Meeting Structure:

- Introductions: If team members are new to one another, allow time for introductions and icebreakers.

Project Overview:

- Purpose: Clearly articulate the "why" behind the project. What problem is it solving? What value will it deliver?
- Goals: Define SMART (Specific, Measurable, Achievable, Relevant, Time-Bound) goals.
- Scope: Outline what's in and what's out of the project.
- Timeline: Present a high-level timeline with key milestones.
- Roles & Responsibilities: Clarify who is doing what.
- Communication Plan: Explain how, when, and where the team will communicate.
- Open Discussion: Encourage questions, concerns, and ideas.
- Next Steps: Define immediate actions and responsibilities.

Additional Tips:

- Keep it Engaging: Use visuals, interactive elements, or a short team-building activity to make the meeting memorable.
- Facilitate, Don't Dominate: Let others participate and contribute.
- Manage Time: Stick to the agenda to prevent the meeting from dragging on.
- Summarize & Document: Recap key decisions and action items. Distribute meeting notes afterward.

Example Agenda

- Welcome and Introductions (10 minutes)
- Icebreaker Activity (Optional) (5 minutes)
- Project Overview (20 minutes)
    - Purpose
    - Goals
    - Scope
    - Timeline
    - Roles & Responsibilities
    - Communication Plan (10 minutes)
    - Open Discussion & Q&A (15 minutes)
    - Next Steps (5 minutes)
    - Wrap-Up (5 minutes)

Post-Meeting Follow-Up

- Distribute meeting notes.
- Set up regular communication channels (project management software, team meetings, etc.).
- Start working on immediate action items.

Bi-Weekly and Monthly Project Review Meetings: Finding the Right Rhythm for Your Project

The frequency of project review meetings is not one-size-fits-all. It should be tailored to the specific project's nature, timeline, complexity, and other factors. Ultimately, the decision of how often to hold these meetings rests at the prime contractor's discretion.

Balancing Frequency and Need

- Early Stages: At the project's outset, when tasks are often more defined and changes less frequent, monthly meetings may suffice. These initial check-ins allow for high-level progress updates and strategic discussions.
- Increasing Complexity: As the project progresses, new challenges may arise, requiring more frequent communication and coordination. The prime contractor might opt for bi-weekly meetings to address emerging issues promptly and maintain project momentum.
- Dynamic Environments: Projects with tight deadlines, evolving requirements, or multiple dependencies often benefit from bi-weekly meetings. The rapid pace of change necessitates closer monitoring and faster decision-making.
- Contractor's Judgment: The prime contractor, with their deep understanding of the project, is best positioned to gauge the appropriate meeting frequency. They can adjust the cadence as needed throughout the project lifecycle.

The Importance of Flexibility

While a set schedule can be helpful, it's important to remain flexible. The prime contractor should be willing to adapt the meeting frequency based on the project's unique needs. If unexpected issues arise or progress stalls, more frequent meetings may be warranted. Conversely, if things are running smoothly, monthly meetings might be sufficient.

Key Considerations for the Prime Contractor

- Project Timeline: Shorter timelines might demand bi-weekly meetings for closer oversight.
- Project Complexity: Projects with many moving parts often benefit from more frequent check-ins.
- Team Communication Needs: Some teams thrive with frequent communication, while others prefer less frequent but more focused interactions.
- Stakeholder Involvement: If stakeholders require regular updates, monthly meetings might be necessary.

Daily Standup Meetings

Daily stand-ups, also known as daily huddles or scrums, are brief, focused meetings designed to keep teams aligned, engaged, and informed. These short check-ins typically last no more than 15 minutes and are held at the same time each day, often at the start of the workday.

Key Benefits

- Collect Daily Site Logs: Site-Specific Insights. Logs from subcontractors provide detailed information about work completed on-site, materials used, labor hours, and any encountered issues.
    - Data-Driven Decision Making: The data collected in logs helps the prime contractor track progress against the schedule, identify trends, and make informed decisions about resource allocation.
    - Documentation for Accountability: Logs serve as a record of daily activities, helping to resolve disputes, manage change orders, and ensure compliance with contract terms.
- Enhanced Communication: Daily stand-ups facilitate open communication among team members, fostering a sense of collaboration and shared responsibility.
- Real-Time Progress Tracking: By sharing tasks and progress updates, the team gains a clear understanding of where the project stands each day.
- Early Identification of Roadblocks: Stand-ups provide a safe space to surface challenges, allowing the team to address them proactively before they escalate into major setbacks.
- Increased Accountability: Knowing that they will be sharing their progress with the team encourages individuals to stay focused and committed to their tasks.
- Improved Team Morale: The regular cadence of communication fosters a sense of camaraderie and shared purpose.

Typical Daily Stand-Up Format

Each team member briefly answers three key questions:

1. What did I accomplish yesterday? (Focus on completed tasks and progress made.)
2. What will I work on today? (Highlights the day's priorities and goals.)
3. Do I have any roadblocks or challenges? (Opens the door for support and problem-solving.)

Tips for Effective Daily Stand-Ups

- Keep it Brief: Stick to the time limit and focus on essential information.
- Stand Up: Literally, standing up during the meeting can help keep it short and focused.
- Stay on Track: Avoid side conversations or in-depth problem-solving. Save those for separate discussions.

- Action-oriented: Identify solutions to roadblocks and assign clear action items.
- Positive Atmosphere: Foster a supportive and collaborative environment.

By incorporating daily stand-ups into your project routine, you can create a more transparent, efficient, and productive team environment. Let me know if you'd like any further refinements or have other questions!

Part Three: Defining Roles and Responsibilities

Clearly defining roles and responsibilities is a fundamental aspect of effective project management in the construction industry. It establishes a framework for accountability, streamlines communication, and minimizes misunderstandings that can lead to costly delays and disputes.

Roles and Responsibilities

- Clarity and Accountability: Clearly defined roles ensure that everyone involved in the project understands their specific tasks, deliverables, and decision-making authority. This fosters a sense of ownership and accountability, promoting the efficient and timely completion of work.
- Effective Communication: When roles are clearly defined, communication becomes more streamlined and targeted. Team members know who to contact for specific questions or concerns, reducing confusion and delays.
- Conflict Prevention: Clearly defined roles help prevent conflicts and misunderstandings by establishing boundaries and expectations for each team member's contributions.
- Improved Decision-Making: Knowing who is responsible for making decisions on specific aspects of the project streamlines the decision-making process and ensures timely action.
- Enhanced Collaboration: When everyone understands their role and how it fits into the bigger picture, it fosters a collaborative environment where team members work together towards shared goals.

Key Steps to Define Roles and Responsibilities

- Identify Key Roles: Start by identifying all the key roles involved in the project, including project managers, architects, engineers, contractors, subcontractors, suppliers, and other stakeholders.
- Develop a Responsibility Matrix: Create a responsibility matrix (e.g., RACI matrix) that outlines the roles and responsibilities for each task or deliverable. The matrix should clearly indicate who is responsible (R), accountable (A), consulted (C), and informed (I) for each task.
- Document Roles and Responsibilities: Document the roles and responsibilities in the contract documents, project plan, and other relevant project documentation. This ensures that everyone has access to information and can refer to it as needed.
- Communicate Clearly: Communicate the defined roles and responsibilities to all project participants. Ensure that everyone understands their role, their authority, and their accountability for specific tasks.
- Regularly Review and Update: As the project progresses, regularly review and update the roles and responsibilities to reflect any changes in scope, schedule, or team composition.

Best Practices for Defining Roles and Responsibilities

- Involve Key Stakeholders: Engage key stakeholders in the process of defining roles and responsibilities to ensure buy-in and alignment with project goals.
- Be Specific: Clearly define the scope of each role, including specific tasks, deliverables, deadlines, and decision-making authority.
- Avoid Overlapping Responsibilities: Ensure that roles are distinct and avoid assigning the same responsibility to multiple individuals, which can lead to confusion and conflict.
- Delegate Authority: Empower team members by delegating authority and decision-making responsibility to the appropriate level.
- Provide Resources and Support: Ensure that team members have the necessary resources, training, and support to fulfill their roles effectively.

Part Four: Defining Roles and Responsibilities

Open and transparent communication is the cornerstone of successful construction projects. It fosters trust, collaboration, and proactive problem-solving, leading to smoother project execution, reduced risks, and improved outcomes for all stakeholders.

Benefits of Open Communication

- Early Issue Identification: Open communication channels encourage team members to raise concerns or potential issues early on, allowing for timely intervention and preventing them from escalating into major problems.
- Proactive Problem-Solving: When communication is transparent, project teams can collaboratively identify and address challenges before they impact the project's timeline or budget.
- Enhanced Collaboration: Open communication fosters a collaborative environment where team members feel comfortable sharing ideas, concerns, and feedback, leading to better decision-making and innovative solutions.
- Increased Trust and Transparency: Transparent communication builds trust among project stakeholders, creating a positive and productive working relationship.
- Reduced Dispute Risk: Open communication helps to prevent misunderstandings and misinterpretations, which can lead to costly disputes and delays.
- Improved Morale and Productivity: When team members feel heard and valued, it boosts morale and motivation, leading to increased productivity and better project outcomes.

Strategies for Fostering Open Communication

- Establish Clear Communication Channels: Define preferred communication methods (e.g., email, phone, meetings) and establish regular communication schedules to ensure everyone is informed and updated on project progress.
- Encourage Open Dialogue: Create a safe and inclusive environment where team members feel comfortable expressing their opinions, concerns, and ideas without fear of retribution.
- Active Listening: Practice active listening by paying full attention to the speaker, asking clarifying questions, and summarizing what you've heard to ensure understanding.
- Regular Meetings: Schedule regular project meetings to discuss progress, address issues, and share information. Encourage participation from all team members.
- Transparency: Be transparent about project decisions, challenges, and changes. Share information openly and honestly to build trust and avoid surprises.
- Feedback Mechanisms: Establish feedback mechanisms, such as surveys or suggestion boxes, to gather input from team members and identify areas for improvement.

- Conflict Resolution: Address conflicts or disagreements promptly and constructively. Encourage open dialogue and seek win-win solutions.
- Technology: To facilitate communication and information sharing, utilize technology tools such as project management software, collaboration platforms, and video conferencing.

Overcoming Barriers to Open Communication

- Fear of Retribution: Create a culture where team members feel safe to speak up without fear of negative consequences.
- Lack of Trust: Build trust through consistent communication, transparency, and follow-through on commitments.
- Hierarchy: Encourage communication across all levels of the project team, regardless of position or title.
- Cultural Differences: Be aware of cultural differences in communication styles, and adapt your approach accordingly.

Part Five: Defining Roles and Responsibilities

In the fast-paced and complex world of construction, issues and conflicts are bound to arise. However, the key to successful project management lies in addressing these issues promptly and effectively before they escalate into costly disputes and claims. By implementing proactive strategies and fostering a culture of open communication, you can minimize disruptions, maintain project momentum, and preserve valuable relationships.

Why Prompt Issue Resolution Matters

- Cost Savings: Addressing issues early on can prevent them from snowballing into larger, more expensive problems that require extensive resources and time to resolve.
- Time Management: Promptly resolving issues helps keep the project on schedule, avoiding delays that can impact deadlines and overall project completion.
- Relationship Preservation: Openly addressing concerns and working collaboratively to find solutions can strengthen relationships between project stakeholders, fostering trust and cooperation.
- Reputation Management: A reputation for proactively addressing issues and resolving disputes amicably can help you stand out in the industry and attract future business opportunities.
- Legal Compliance: Many contracts require timely notification and resolution of issues to avoid potential breaches or waivers of rights.

Strategies for Prompt Issue Resolution

- Early Identification: Establish a system for identifying potential issues early on, such as regular progress meetings, site inspections, and open communication channels for team members to raise concerns.
- Open Communication: Encourage open and honest communication among all project stakeholders. Create a safe environment where individuals feel comfortable raising concerns without fear of retribution.
- Collaborative Problem-Solving: When an issue arises, bring together the relevant parties to discuss the problem and brainstorm potential solutions together. Focus on finding win-win solutions that address the needs of all stakeholders.
- Timely Decision-Making: Avoid delays in decision-making. Establish clear timelines for addressing issues and ensure that decisions are made promptly and communicated to all relevant parties.
- Documentation: Document all issues, discussions, decisions, and actions taken to resolve the problem. This documentation can be valuable in the event of future disputes or misunderstandings.

- Escalation Process: Establish a clear escalation process for issues that cannot be resolved at the initial level. This may involve bringing in higher-level management or utilizing alternative dispute resolution methods, such as mediation or arbitration.

Additional Tips for Effective Issue Resolution

- Focus on Interests, Not Positions: Instead of focusing on entrenched positions, try to understand the underlying interests and needs of each party involved in the dispute. This can help identify common ground and facilitate mutually beneficial solutions.
- Be Solution-Oriented: Focus on finding practical and workable solutions rather than dwelling on blame or past mistakes.
- Maintain Professionalism: Even in challenging situations, maintain a professional and respectful demeanor. Avoid personal attacks or inflammatory language.
- Seek Mediation or Facilitation: If direct negotiations are unsuccessful, consider engaging a neutral third party, such as a mediator or facilitator, to help guide the discussion and facilitate a resolution.

Module 6: Preparing, Drafting, and Defending Claims

Claims are an unfortunate reality in the complex world of construction. They can arise from unforeseen events, changes in project scope, delays, or disagreements over contract interpretation. Module 6 delves into the intricacies of preparing, drafting, and defending claims in the construction industry. This module equips project managers and executives with the knowledge and skills to navigate the complexities of claims, ensuring that their interests are protected and that disputes are resolved efficiently and fairly.

Part One: Preparing for Claims. This section emphasizes the importance of proactive claim preparation. It explores the various types of claims that can arise in construction projects, the common causes of claims, and the potential impact of claims on project outcomes. You'll learn how to identify potential claim scenarios, gather and organize documentation, track costs and delays, and develop a comprehensive claim strategy. By preparing for claims in advance, you can minimize their negative impact and maximize your chances of a successful resolution.

Part Two: Drafting Effective Claim Documents. Crafting clear, concise, and persuasive claim documents is crucial for a successful resolution. This section provides a step-by-step guide to drafting effective claim documents, including notice letters, claim letters, and supporting documentation. You'll learn about the key principles of effective claim drafting, such as clarity, specificity, factual accuracy, organization, persuasiveness, and professionalism. Mastering the art of claim drafting allows you to present your case convincingly and increases your chances of recovery.

Part Three: Responding to and Defending Against Claims. Responding to and defending against claims requires a strategic and well-informed approach. This section explores various strategies for responding to claims, including conducting thorough reviews, analyzing contract provisions, investigating the claims, evaluating their validity, and developing a response strategy. You'll also learn how to defend against claims by gathering evidence, preparing counterclaims, and utilizing dispute resolution mechanisms such as mediation or arbitration. By understanding the intricacies of claim defense, you can protect your interests and minimize potential losses.

Part Four: Case Studies and Practical Exercises. This section provides real-world case studies and practical exercises to reinforce your understanding of claim preparation, drafting, and defense. You'll analyze actual claim scenarios, develop response strategies, and practice drafting claim documents. These exercises will help you apply the knowledge and skills learned in this module to real-world situations, preparing you to effectively manage claims and disputes in your construction projects.

Part One: Preparing for Claims

Construction claims are formal requests for additional compensation, time extensions, or other remedies for unforeseen events, changes, or disputes that arise during a project. While claims are sometimes unavoidable, proactive preparation can significantly increase the chances of a successful resolution and minimize the negative impact on project outcomes.

Understanding Construction Claims

- Types of Claims: Construction claims can be categorized into various types, including delay claims, disruption claims, acceleration claims, defective work claims, and payment claims. Each type of claim has specific requirements and considerations.
- Causes of Claims: Claims can arise from a variety of factors, such as design errors, unforeseen site conditions, owner-caused delays, changes in scope, or differing interpretations of contract terms.
- Impact of Claims: Claims can lead to costly disputes, project delays, strained relationships, and financial losses for all parties involved.

Proactive Claim Preparation

- Know Your Contract: Thoroughly understand the contract terms and conditions, including the notice provisions, change order procedures, dispute resolution mechanisms, and any clauses related to claims or time extensions.
- Identify Potential Claim Scenarios: Proactively identify potential risks and issues that could lead to claims. This may involve conducting risk assessments, reviewing project plans and specifications, and monitoring project progress for early warning signs of potential problems.
- Gather and Organize Documentation: Maintain meticulous records of all project-related documents, including contracts, change orders, correspondence, meeting minutes, daily reports, photos, videos, and any other relevant information. Organize these documents in a clear and easily accessible manner.
- Track Costs and Delays: Keep detailed records of all costs incurred and delays experienced due to unforeseen events or changes. This documentation will be crucial in substantiating your claim and calculating damages.
- Communicate Proactively: Keep open and transparent with the owner and other project stakeholders. Notify them promptly of any potential issues or delays, and document all communications.
- Follow Notice Requirements: For any potential claims, comply with the contractually mandated notice requirements. Failure to provide timely notice can result in a waiver of rights or remedies.
- Develop a Claim Strategy: If a claim becomes necessary, develop a clear and comprehensive claim strategy. This should include identifying the legal basis for the

claim, calculating damages, gathering supporting evidence, and determining the desired outcome.

- Seek Legal Counsel: If the claim is complex or involves significant financial or legal implications, consult with an attorney specializing in construction law. They can provide guidance on claim preparation, negotiation, and potential litigation strategies.

Additional Tips for Claim Preparation

- Be Thorough: Ensure that your claim is well-supported by documentation and evidence.
- Be Realistic: Be realistic in your assessment of damages and avoid exaggerating your claims.
- Be Professional: In all communications and negotiations related to the claim, maintain a professional and respectful tone.
- Be Prepared to Negotiate: Be willing to negotiate and compromise in order to reach a mutually agreeable resolution.

Part Two: Drafting Effective Claim Documents

In the construction industry, claims are formal requests for additional compensation, time extensions, or other remedies due to unforeseen events, changes, or disputes that arise during a project. Crafting clear, concise, and persuasive claim documents is crucial for a successful resolution and maximizing your chances of recovery.

Types of Claim Documents

- Notice Letters: These are the initial notifications sent to the other party, informing them of the issue and your intent to seek a remedy.
- Claim Letters: These provide a detailed explanation of the claim, including the factual and contractual basis, the impact on the project, and the damages sought.
- Supporting Documentation: This includes any evidence that supports your claim, such as contracts, change orders, correspondence, photos, videos, expert reports, and daily logs.

Key Principles of Effective Claim Drafting

- Clarity: Use clear and concise language, avoiding jargon and technical terms that the recipient may not understand.
- Specificity: Clearly identify the issue, the relevant contractual provisions, the impact on the project, and the specific relief sought.
- Factual Accuracy: Ensure that all information presented is accurate, verifiable, and supported by evidence.
- Organization: Present your claim in a logical and organized manner, using headings and subheadings to guide the reader.
- Persuasiveness: Use persuasive language and arguments to convince the recipient of the validity of your claim and the reasonableness of your requested relief.
- Professionalism: Throughout the document, maintain a professional and respectful tone, even if you express disagreement or frustration.

Drafting Notice Letters

- Timeliness: Send notice letters promptly after the issue arises to avoid waiving any rights or remedies.
- Content: Clearly state the purpose of the notice, the issue or breach of contract, and your intent to seek a remedy.
- Conciseness: Keep the notice letter brief and to the point, focusing on the essential information.

Drafting Claim Letters

- Introduction: Provide a brief summary of the claim and the relief sought.

- Factual Background: Provide a detailed account of the events or circumstances leading to the claim, including dates, project references, and supporting evidence.
- Contractual Basis: Cite the specific contractual provisions that support your claim.
- Impact and Damages: Quantify the issue's impact on the project and provide a detailed breakdown of the damages sought.
- Conclusion: Reiterate your request for relief and propose a course of action for resolution.

Supporting Documentation

- Organization: Use tabs or dividers to separate different types of supporting documents in a clear and logical manner.
- Relevance: Include only documents that are directly related to the claim.
- Authentication: Ensure that all documents are authentic and can be verified if necessary.

Additional Tips

- Seek Legal Counsel: If the claim is complex or involves significant financial or legal implications, consult with an attorney specializing in construction law.
- Negotiation: Be prepared to negotiate with the other party to reach a mutually agreeable resolution.
- Alternative Dispute Resolution: Consider using alternative dispute resolution methods, such as mediation or arbitration, to avoid costly litigation.

Part Three: Responding to and Defending Against Claims

In the construction industry, claims are a common occurrence, arising from unforeseen events, changes in scope, or disagreements over contract interpretation. Responding to and defending against claims effectively is crucial for protecting your interests, minimizing financial losses, and preserving relationships with project stakeholders.

Understanding Claims

- Types of Claims: Construction claims can be categorized into various types, including delay claims, disruption claims, acceleration claims, defective work claims, and payment claims. Each type of claim has specific requirements and considerations.
- Causes of Claims: Claims can arise from a variety of factors, such as design errors, unforeseen site conditions, owner-caused delays, changes in scope, or differing interpretations of contract terms.
- Impact of Claims: Claims can lead to costly disputes, project delays, strained relationships, and financial losses for all parties involved.

Strategies for Responding to Claims

- Thorough Review: Carefully review the claim documents, including the notice letter, claim letter, and any supporting documentation. Identify the specific issues raised, the claimed damages, and the legal basis for the claim.
- Contractual Analysis: Review the relevant contract provisions to determine the rights and obligations of each party, the notice requirements, and the dispute resolution procedures.
- Investigation: Conduct a thorough investigation of the claim, gathering evidence to support your position. This may involve reviewing project records, interviewing witnesses, consulting with experts, and conducting site inspections.
- Evaluation: Assess the validity of the claim based on the contract terms, the evidence gathered, and applicable legal principles. Determine your position's strengths and weaknesses, as well as the potential risks and costs of the claim.
- Response Strategy: Develop a clear and comprehensive response strategy. This may involve negotiating a settlement, preparing a counterclaim, or defending against the claim in mediation, arbitration, or litigation.
- Communication: Maintain open and professional communication with the claimant throughout the process. Clearly articulate your position, provide supporting evidence, and explore potential solutions.

Defending Against Claims

- Early Intervention: To prevent potential issues from escalating into formal claims, address them early on.
- Documentation: Maintain meticulous records of all project-related activities, including daily reports, correspondence, meeting minutes, and change orders.

- Contractual Compliance: Strictly adhere to the terms of the contract, including notice provisions, change order procedures, and payment terms.
- Risk Management: Identify and mitigate potential risks that could lead to claims, such as design errors, unforeseen site conditions, or material shortages.
- Legal Counsel: Consult with an attorney specializing in construction law to assess the merits of the claim and develop a defense strategy.

Negotiating a Fair Resolution

- Focus on Interests: Identify the underlying interests and needs of both parties and seek solutions that address those interests.
- Openness to Compromise: Be willing to compromise and explore creative solutions that meet the needs of both parties.
- Mediation or Arbitration: Consider using mediation or arbitration as a less adversarial and more cost-effective alternative to litigation.

Part Four: Case Studies and Practical Exercises

The following case studies present real-world scenarios involving contract disputes in the construction industry. Each case study includes key documents, such as contracts, correspondence, and expert reports, to provide a comprehensive understanding of the issues involved. Participants are assigned roles as either the owner, contractor, subcontractor, supplier, or neutral observer, and are tasked with analyzing the situation, developing arguments, and proposing solutions based on their assigned perspective. The case studies are designed to be interactive and engaging, encouraging participants to apply the knowledge and skills they have learned throughout the modules to real-world scenarios. By working through these case studies, participants will gain valuable experience in contract interpretation, risk management, dispute resolution, and effective communication in the construction industry.

Case Study 1: Delay Claim

ABC Contracting (the general contractor) awarded a subcontract to Best One Services (the subcontractor) for foundation work on a private middle school project. The project faced time constraints, and ABC Contracting chose Best One Services based solely on the lowest bid without conducting thorough due diligence (e.g., reference checks, financial stability assessment, insurance verification, or performance bond requirements). The contractor's project manager and team liked the subcontractor's project manager and believed he was the best person for the job.

During excavation, Best One Services encountered unforeseen conditions that caused delays and cost overruns. Their initial communication via email was informal and lacked sufficient detail. In response, ABC Contracting requested additional documentation to substantiate the claim, which the subcontractor perceived as a delaying tactic. The situation escalated, with the subcontractor threatening to stop work unless their demands were met.

Time : 45 minutes

Key Documents:

1. Initial Email
2. Construction Services Subcontract
3. Response to Claim Formal Letter
4. Subcontractor's Email Response
5. Formal Response to Claim

Instructions for Teams:

Team 1 (Subcontractor/Best One Services):

- Analyze the situation: Carefully review the initial email, the subcontract agreement, and the subsequent correspondence. Identify the specific clauses in the contract that support your claim for additional time and compensation.
- Gather Evidence: Determine what additional documentation you can provide to strengthen your case, such as daily reports, photos, expert opinions, or any records of communication with the general contractor regarding the unforeseen conditions.
- Develop Arguments: Prepare arguments highlighting why you believe you are entitled to the additional time and compensation. Focus on the impact of the unforeseen conditions on your work, the lack of adequate notice or support from the general contractor, and any potential breaches of contract on their part.
- Consider Dispute Resolution: Evaluate the potential risks and benefits of pursuing different dispute resolution methods, such as negotiation, mediation, or arbitration. Determine your preferred approach based on your priorities and your case's strengths.
- Present Your Case: Select a spokesperson to present your arguments to the class clearly and persuasively. Be prepared to address potential counterarguments from the general contractor and defend your position.

Team 2 (General Contractor/ABC Contracting):

- You've just stepped into your new role as project manager for ABC Contracting on the private middle school project. Your predecessor left abruptly for another company, leaving you with an escalating dispute with Best One Services, the subcontractor responsible for foundation work. Your immediate task is to get up to speed on the situation, review the formal correspondence exchanged so far, and devise a strategy to resolve this dispute effectively.
    - Review contractual obligations: Thoroughly examine the subcontract agreement to identify clauses that support your position, such as the requirement for detailed documentation of claims, the notice requirements for unforeseen conditions, and the limitation of liability clause.
    - Assess the Evidence: Evaluate the evidence provided by the subcontractor, including their initial email, any daily reports, and any additional documentation they submit. Determine whether it meets the contractual requirements for substantiating a claim.
    - Develop Counterarguments: Prepare arguments to refute the subcontractor's claim, focusing on their failure to provide adequate documentation, their lack of adherence to contractual procedures, and any potential breaches of contract on their part (e.g., the threat to stop work).
    - Explore Resolution Options: Consider different options for resolving the dispute, such as negotiating a settlement, engaging in mediation or arbitration, or potentially terminating the subcontract if the subcontractor refuses to perform. Weigh the risks and benefits of each option.
    - Present your Defense: Choose a spokesperson to present your arguments to the class, clearly outlining your contractual obligations, the deficiencies in the subcontractor's claim, and your proposed resolution strategy.

Team 3 (Neutral Observers):

- Analyze Both Sides: Carefully review all the documents and listen to the arguments presented by both the owner and the supply company. Identify the strengths and weaknesses of each side's case.
- Assess Contractual Compliance: Determine whether both parties have fulfilled their contractual obligations. Consider the clarity of the contract language, the adequacy of the subcontractor's documentation, and the general contractor's adherence to the dispute resolution process.
- Identify Areas of Compromise: Explore potential areas where both parties could find common ground, such as a revised payment schedule, a partial waiver of damages, or an agreement on future communication protocols.
- Propose a Fair Resolution: Based on your analysis, develop a fair and reasonable resolution to the dispute that addresses the concerns of both parties and promotes a successful outcome for the project.
- Present Your Findings: Share your analysis and recommendations with the class, highlighting the key legal and contractual issues, the strengths and weaknesses of each side's arguments, and your proposed path to resolution.

Case Materials

Initial e-mail

Initial email from Best One Services to ABC Contracting:

> John,
>
> Just wanted to let you guys know we're running behind schedule. Stuff came up during excavation that slowed us down, and now we need two more weeks to finish.
>
> Also, because of this, it's gonna cost you an extra $40,000.I am adding this to the change log and sending you an invoice. I need it paid as soon as you receive it.
>
> Thanks,
>
> Robert

Construction Services Subcontract

(Example for training. Do not use)

This Subcontract Agreement ("Agreement") is made and entered into as of this [Date] day of [Month], [Year], by and between:

ABC Contracting, a [State] company with its principal place of business at [Address], hereinafter referred to as "Contractor,"

Best One Services, a [State] company with its principal place of business at [Address], hereinafter referred to as "Subcontractor."

WITNESSETH:

WHEREAS, Contractor has entered into a contract with [Owner Name] (the "Prime Contract") for the construction of [Project Name] located at [Project Address] (the "Project"); and

WHEREAS, Contractor desires to engage Subcontractor to perform certain work on the Project, as more particularly described herein;

NOW, THEREFORE, in consideration of the mutual covenants and promises contained herein, the parties agree as follows:

1. SCOPE OF WORK

Subcontractor shall furnish all labor, materials, equipment, tools, supervision, and other items necessary to complete the construction of the foundations for the Project in accordance with the plans, specifications, and other documents referenced in the Prime Contract (collectively, the "Contract Documents"). The contract price is a firm-fixed price and is inclusive of the entire Scope of Work described herein. No changes to the Scope of Work shall be made unless agreed upon in writing by both parties prior to the commencement of such work.

2. UNFORESEEN CONDITIONS

In the event that Subcontractor encounters any unforeseen site conditions or obstructions during the performance of its work, Subcontractor shall immediately stop work in the affected area and notify Contractor in writing of such conditions. Subcontractor shall not proceed with any work affected by the unforeseen conditions until directed to do so by Contractor.

3. PAYMENT

Contractor shall pay Subcontractor for the satisfactory performance of the work in accordance with the schedule of values approved by Contractor, within thirty (30) days after Contractor receives payment from the Owner for the Subcontractor's work.

4. TAXES

Subcontractor shall be solely responsible for all taxes, fees, or other governmental charges that may be levied or assessed in connection with the work performed under this Agreement.

5. NOTICES

All notices, requests, demands, or other communications required or permitted to be given under this Agreement shall be in writing and shall be deemed to have been duly given when delivered personally or by certified mail, return receipt requested, to the respective parties at their addresses set forth above.

6. INDEMNIFICATION

Subcontractor shall indemnify, defend, and hold harmless Contractor and its officers, directors, employees, agents, and representatives from and against any and all claims, damages, losses, liabilities, expenses, and costs, including reasonable attorneys' fees, arising out of or resulting from the performance of the work under this Agreement, provided that such claim, damage, loss, or liability is attributable to bodily injury, sickness, disease, or death, or to injury to or destruction of tangible property (other than the Work itself) including the loss of use resulting therefrom, to the extent caused in whole or in part by any negligent act or omission of Subcontractor, or anyone directly or indirectly employed by them or anyone for whose acts they may be liable, regardless of whether or not such claim, damage, loss, or liability is caused in part by a party indemnified hereunder.

7. LIMITATION OF LIABILITY

Neither party shall be liable to the other for any consequential, incidental, indirect, special, or punitive damages arising out of or relating to this Agreement, regardless of the cause of action or theory of liability.

8. SAFETY

Subcontractor shall comply with all applicable safety regulations and shall take all reasonable precautions for the safety of employees on the Project. Subcontractor shall be responsible for any violations of safety regulations and any injuries or damage resulting from such violations.

9. CLAIMS

All claims by Subcontractor for additional time or compensation must be submitted in writing to Contractor within [Number] days of the event giving rise to the claim. The claim must be supported by documentation acceptable to Contractor that substantiates the costs and time incurred. The claim must also be approved by the Owner. Contractor's determination of the validity and amount of any claim shall be final and binding.

10. GOVERNING LAW AND VENUE

This Agreement shall be governed by and construed in accordance with the laws of the State of Delaware, without regard to its conflict of law provisions. Any dispute arising out of or relating to this Agreement shall be resolved in the state or federal courts located in [County/City], Delaware.

11. DISPUTE RESOLUTION

Any dispute arising out of or relating to this Agreement shall be resolved in the following manner:

a. Step 1: The Project Managers for Contractor and Subcontractor shall attempt in good faith to resolve the dispute within [Number] days of written notice of the dispute.

b. Step 2: If the dispute is not resolved in Step 1, the Program Managers for Contractor and Subcontractor shall attempt in good faith to resolve the dispute within [Number] days.

c. Step 3: If the dispute is not resolved in Step 2, the executives designated by Contractor and Subcontractor shall attempt in good faith to resolve the dispute within [Number] days.

d. Step 4: If the dispute is not resolved in Step 3, either party may submit the dispute to binding arbitration in accordance with the rules of the [Arbitration Organization Name]. The arbitration shall be held in [City, State].

IN WITNESS WHEREOF, the parties have executed this Agreement as of the date first written above.

Response to Claim Formal Letter

RE: Notice of Delay and Claim for Additional Compensation - [Project Name]

This letter is in response to your email submitted on [Date of Email] titled "[Subject line]" regarding a delay and claim for additional compensation due to unforeseen site conditions encountered during the excavation phase of the [Project Name] project.

We acknowledge receipt of your notification and appreciate you bringing this matter to our attention. However, after careful review, we find that the information provided is insufficient to fully assess the impact of the unforeseen conditions on the project schedule and cost.

As outlined in Clause 9 of our Subcontract Agreement, we require a more comprehensive and detailed account of the following:

Detailed Description of Unforeseen Conditions: Please provide a thorough description of the specific site conditions encountered, including their precise location(s), nature (e.g., type of rock, soil composition, unexpected utilities), and how they deviate from the conditions represented in the Contract Documents.

Specific Impact on Work: Clearly articulate how these unforeseen conditions directly impacted your work, including specific tasks affected, disruptions to planned activities, and any necessary changes in work methods or sequencing.

Quantified Delay Analysis: To substantiate the claimed delay, please submit a detailed critical path method (CPM) schedule analysis. This analysis should illustrate the specific activities impacted, the duration of each delay, and the cumulative impact on the overall project schedule.

Itemized Cost Breakdown: Provide a comprehensive breakdown of all costs incurred as a direct result of the unforeseen conditions. This should include invoices, receipts, and other supporting documentation for labor, equipment, materials, and any other relevant expenses, clearly linked to the specific conditions encountered.

Expert Reports (if applicable): If you have engaged any experts to assess the unforeseen conditions or the resulting delays and costs, please provide copies of their reports or findings.

Please be advised that your claim, in its current state, does not meet the requirements outlined in Clause 9 of our Subcontract Agreement. Therefore, we are unable to initiate the review process with the Owner at this time.

While we await the requested documentation, we have logged this issue in our project records. However, please note that until a comprehensive evaluation has been conducted, and the Owner has had the opportunity to review and render a decision, this matter will not be considered a formal change order.

We request your prompt cooperation in providing the additional information outlined above. This will enable us to expedite the evaluation of your claim and work towards a mutually agreeable resolution. We value our partnership and are committed to collaborating with you to address this issue effectively and ensure the successful completion of the project.

Please do not hesitate to contact us if you have any questions or require further clarification.

Subcontractor's e-mail Response

John,

We've given you everything you need to assess our claim. We have been giving you daily reports since we started the project. You need to look at them.

Demanding more paperwork is just a stall tactic, and we're not playing that game. You've been paid for our work, and now you're refusing to cover the extra costs caused by those surprise conditions. That's a breach of our contract, plain and simple.

We're stopping all work on the project until we get paid what we're owed. You need to bring a check for $[Amount] to the site by [Time] on [Date]. If that doesn't happen, we'll see this as another breach and take further action.

Get this sorted out. We're ready to talk, but not until we're paid.

Thanks,

Robert

Formal Response to Claim

RE: Rejection of Delay and Claim for Additional Compensation - [Project Name]

Dear [Subcontractor Contact Person],

This letter is in response to your email dated [Date of Email] titled "[Subject line]" regarding your claim for additional compensation and time extension due to unforeseen site conditions encountered during the excavation phase of the [Project Name] project.

We have reviewed your initial notification, subsequent correspondence, and your recent threat to stop work if your demands are not met. Please be advised that any unauthorized work stoppage on your part will be considered a material breach of our Subcontract Agreement. Such a breach will entitle us to take appropriate actions, including but not limited to:

- Termination of your subcontract for default.
- Backcharging you for any damages incurred as a result of the work stoppage.
- Engaging another subcontractor to complete your scope of work at your expense.

Regarding your claim, despite our repeated requests for additional information and documentation as required by Clause 9 of our Subcontract Agreement, you have failed to provide sufficient evidence to substantiate your claim. Specifically, we have not received:

- Detailed daily reports from the period when the unforeseen conditions were encountered.
- A quantified delay analysis demonstrating the specific impact on the project schedule.
- An itemized cost breakdown with supporting documentation clearly linking the claimed costs to the unforeseen conditions.
- Expert reports (if applicable) to corroborate your assertions.

Furthermore, it appears you did not adhere to the procedures outlined in Clause 2 of our Agreement regarding unforeseen conditions. Upon encountering such conditions, you were required to immediately stop work in the affected area and notify us in writing. We have no record of this notification until your initial claim email.

Given your failure to provide the necessary documentation and follow contractual procedures, we must formally reject your claim for additional time and compensation.

This decision is without prejudice to your right to submit a revised claim with the required documentation and in compliance with the terms of our Agreement. However, we strongly encourage you to promptly provide the requested information to facilitate a timely resolution of this matter.

Should you wish to dispute this decision, you are free to initiate the dispute resolution process outlined in Section 11 of our Subcontract Agreement. However, any unauthorized work stoppage will be considered a separate breach of contract and will be dealt with accordingly.

We urge you to reconsider your position and continue performing your work under the contract. We are open to further discussion once you have provided the necessary documentation to support your claim.

ABC Contracting reserves all rights and remedies in this matter.

Discussion Questions

1. **What risks did ABC Contracting take by not conducting thorough due diligence on Best One Services before awarding the subcontract?**

____

____

____

____

2. **Does the subcontract adequately address unforeseen conditions and change orders? If not, what specific language should be added or improved?**

____

____

____

____

3. **How could both parties have improved their communication to de-escalate the situation and reach a resolution? What strategies and tools could prevent future misunderstandings?**

____

____

____

____

4. **What dispute resolution options are available per the contract, and what are their pros and cons for each party? When should legal counsel be involved?**

____

____

____

____

5. **Did either party act unethically or unprofessionally? What ethical principles should guide contractors and subcontractors in such situations?**

____

____

____

____

6. **What lessons can be learned from this case study, and what preventive measures could avoid similar disputes and foster better collaboration?**

____

____

____

____

Notes:

Case Study 2: Defective Equipment Claim

Your company, a supplier of specialized mining equipment, successfully delivered an order to a customer. However, due to unforeseen circumstances involving third-party contractors, the equipment remained uninstalled and exposed to the elements for eight months. Upon installation, the customer discovered significant rust and corrosion, rendering the equipment inoperable. The customer has sent a formal notice demanding repair, replacement, and compensation for substantial daily losses.

Time : 45 minutes

Key Documents:

1. Notice Letter
2. Supply and Services Agreement
3. Operations and Maintenance Manual
4. Engineer's Report with Pictures

Instructions for Teams:

- Team 1 (Owner): After answering the discussion questions, prepare a strong case for why the company is liable for the damage and should compensate the customer for their losses. Focus on the contractual obligations, the O&M manual instructions, and any potential negligence on the company's part.
- Team 2 (Supply Company): After answering the discussion questions, develop a defense strategy, considering the contract terms, the evidence at hand, and potential arguments for shared responsibility or limited liability.
- Team 3 (Neutral Observers): After answering the discussion questions, analyze the strengths and weaknesses of each side's arguments, identify potential areas of compromise, and propose a fair and reasonable resolution to the dispute.

Notice Letter

Subject : Defective Equipment and Incurred Damages

This letter serves as formal notification that the equipment purchased from your company on [Purchase Date] and delivered on [Delivery Date] has been found to be defective. Upon installation on [Installation Date], significant rust and corrosion were discovered inside the equipment, rendering it inoperable.

As a direct result of this defect, we have been forced to shut down our plant operations. We are currently incurring damages of $100,000 per day due to lost production and associated costs.

We demand that you take immediate action to remedy this defect. This includes, but is not limited to, the following:

- Repair or Replacement: The defective equipment must be repaired to a fully functional state or replaced with a new unit.

- Compensation: You are responsible for compensating us for all damages incurred as a result of the defective equipment, including the daily losses of $100,000.

We expect a prompt response to this notice and a detailed plan for rectifying the situation. Failure to take immediate action will leave us no choice but to pursue all available legal remedies to protect our interests.

Supply and Services Agreement

This Supply and Services Agreement ("Agreement") is made and entered into as of this [Date] day of [Month], [Year], by and between:

ABC Contracting, a [State] company with its principal place of business at [Address], hereinafter referred to as "Contractor,"

Best One Supply and Services, a [State] company with its principal place of business at [Address], hereinafter referred to as "Supplier."

WITNESSETH:

WHEREAS, Contractor has entered into a contract with [Owner Name] (the "Prime Contract") for the construction of [Project Name] located at [Project Address] (the "Project"); and

WHEREAS, Contractor desires to engage Supplier to provide certain equipment ("Equipment") on the Project, as more particularly described herein;

NOW, THEREFORE, in consideration of the mutual covenants and promises contained herein, the parties agree as follows:

1. SCOPE OF WORK

Supplier shall furnish all labor, materials, Equipment, tools, supervision, and other items necessary and in accordance with the plans, specifications, and other documents referenced in the Prime Contract (collectively, the "Contract Documents"). The contract price is a firm-fixed price and is inclusive of the entire Scope of Work described herein. No changes to the Scope of Work shall be made unless agreed upon in writing by both parties prior to the commencement of such work.

1. PAYMENT

Contractor shall pay Supplier thirty (30) days after receipt of the Equipment.

2. TAXES

Supplier shall be solely responsible for all taxes, fees, or other governmental charges that may be levied or assessed in connection with the Equipment under this Agreement.

3. NOTICES

All notices, requests, demands, or other communications required or permitted to be given under this Agreement shall be in writing and shall be deemed to have been duly given when delivered personally or by certified mail, return receipt requested, to the respective parties at their addresses set forth above.

4. INDEMNIFICATION

Supplier shall indemnify, defend, and hold harmless Contractor and its officers, directors, employees, agents, and representatives from and against any and all claims, damages, losses, liabilities, expenses, and costs, including reasonable attorneys' fees, arising out of or resulting from the performance of the work under this Agreement, provided that such claim, damage, loss, or liability is attributable to bodily injury, sickness, disease, or death, or to injury to or destruction of tangible property (other than the Work itself) including the loss of use resulting therefrom, to the extent caused in whole or in part by any negligent act or omission of Supplier, or anyone directly or indirectly employed by them or anyone for whose acts they may be liable, regardless of whether or not such claim, damage, loss, or liability is caused in part by a party indemnified hereunder.

5. WARRANTY

Supplier warrants that all materials and workmanship furnished under this Agreement will be free from defects for a period of one (1) year from the date of delivery of the Equipment. Supplier's sole obligation under this warranty shall be to repair or replace, at its option, any defective materials or workmanship within a reasonable time after receipt of written notice from Contractor. Prior to installation, Customer shall be responsible for the proper storage of all Equipment furnished by Supplier in accordance with manufacturer recommendations and industry best practices. Customer shall also operate and maintain all Equipment in accordance with the Operation and Maintenance Manuals provided by Supplier. Failure to properly store, operate, or maintain the equipment may void this warranty.

6. LIMITATION OF LIABILITY

Neither party shall be liable to the other for any consequential, incidental, indirect, special, or punitive damages arising out of or relating to this Agreement, regardless of the cause of action or theory of liability. This includes, but is not limited to, lost profits, loss of business, loss of data, plant shutdowns, or other losses arising from any plant shutdown, whether foreseeable or unforeseeable. In no event shall the total liability of either party to the other exceed the total amount paid by the Contractor to the Supplier under this Agreement.

7. GOVERNING LAW AND VENUE

This Agreement shall be governed by and construed in accordance with the laws of the State of Delaware, without regard to its conflict of law provisions. Any claim or dispute arising out of or relating to this Agreement shall be resolved exclusively in the state or federal courts located in Delaware. The parties hereby irrevocably consent to the exclusive jurisdiction and venue of such courts.

Operations and Maintenance Manual

Important Notice:

The procedures outlined in this manual are crucial for the safe and efficient operation of your equipment. Failure to adhere to these guidelines may result in significant damage, premature wear, or even complete equipment failure. The owner assumes full responsibility for any damage incurred due to improper use or maintenance.

Section 1: Storage and Handling

1.1 Shipping: Your equipment is shipped in protective packaging to prevent damage during transit. Please inspect the equipment thoroughly upon receipt for any signs of damage.

1.2 Long-Term Storage: If the equipment is not to be used immediately, it must be stored indoors in a clean, dry environment. If indoor storage is not possible, the equipment must be completely wrapped and sealed to protect it from the elements, including rain, snow, direct sunlight, and extreme temperatures.

Section 2: Initial Lubrication

2.1 Gearbox Oil: The gearbox is shipped with a minimal amount of oil to prevent rust during transit. We have included the additional oil with the gearbox. It is imperative to fill the gearbox completely with the manufacturer-recommended oil (only) upon receipt of the equipment. Failure to do so may result in corrosion and premature wear of the gears.

2.2 Oil Level Check: Regularly check the oil level in the gearbox and top up as needed. Refer to the manufacturer's instructions for the recommended oil type and fill level.

Section 3: Long-Term Idling

3.1 Gear Rotation: If the equipment is expected to remain idle for more than 90 days, it is essential to have a qualified engineer open the gearbox and inspect the gears. The gears must then be rotated manually by at least a quarter turn to prevent rust and ensure proper lubrication distribution.

3.2 Re-lubrication: After rotating the gears, ensure the gearbox is filled to the correct level with fresh oil. There is an oil level indicator on the side of the gearbox.

Engineers Report

Best Engineering was retained by ABC Supply Company to conduct an on-site inspection of a gearbox at their customer's mining operation. During the inspection, it was observed that the hatch cover watertight gaskets were misaligned, and the manufacturer's seal was broken. Upon opening the gearbox, a significant accumulation of water (approximately 2 inches) was found at the bottom of the unit. Additionally, substantial rust was present on the sprockets. While the gearbox could still be rotated, excessive force was required.

The owner's representative indicated that they had become aware of potential issues due to loud noises emanating from the gearboxes during operation. Based on the observed conditions and operational feedback, it is my professional opinion as an engineer that the gearbox has sustained significant damage and cannot be adequately repaired on-site. I recommend that the gearbox be returned to the manufacturer for comprehensive assessment and potential refurbishment or replacement. See attached pictures.

Discussion Questions

1. **What steps should the supply company take upon receiving the notice letter?** Consider internal investigation, communication with the customer, and potential involvement of legal counsel.

2. **How should the company investigate the claim? What evidence should be gathered (e.g., photos, maintenance logs, weather records)? Should experts be consulted?**

3. **What are the most likely causes of the rust and corrosion? Was it solely due to the prolonged outdoor storage, or could other factors (e.g., manufacturing defects, improper initial lubrication) have contributed?**

4. **Does the contract explicitly address:**
    a. Packing and delivery?
    b. Responsibility for storage during delays?
    c. The customer's obligation to mitigate damages?
    d. Limitations of liability for consequential damages?

2. **What arguments could the company make to defend against the customer's claim?** Could they argue force majeure due to the third-party delays? Could they invoke the warranty limitations or argue that the customer failed to properly store the equipment as per the O&M manual?

____

____

____

____

3. **Were there any discussions or agreements between the company and the customer regarding storage arrangements during the delay?**

____

____

____

____

4. **Did the company provide any guidance or assistance to the customer regarding storage or interim maintenance?**

____

____

____

____

5. **Does the engineer's report definitively rule out any manufacturing defects as contributing factors to the damage?**

____

____

____

____

6. **What are the industry standards for storing and maintaining similar equipment during extended delays?**

7. **What was the class's final decision?**

Notes:

“The purpose of this letter is to acknowledge receipt of your claim letter dated [Date of Claim Letter] concerning the condition of the purchased equipment. We understand your concerns regarding the rust and corrosion found on the equipment and the subsequent impact on your operations. To fully assess the situation, we are dispatching a team of engineers to your site to conduct a thorough root cause analysis of the reported defects. We kindly request your cooperation in granting our engineers full access to the equipment for this investigation. If you have any questions or require further information, please do not hesitate to contact me directly.”

To obtain an impartial evaluation of the reported defects and their underlying causes, consider hiring an independent engineering firm to conduct a thorough root cause analysis. This will provide an objective assessment of the equipment's condition, identify any factors contributing to the rust and corrosion. Additionally, engage legal counsel to maintain attorney-client privilege and ensure appropriate responses throughout this process.

Case Study 3: Nonconforming Work and Delay Notice

ABC Construction, the general contractor on a large commercial building project, has engaged XYZ Electrical as a subcontractor to perform all electrical installations. The subcontract between the two parties includes a detailed scope of work, a clearly defined completion deadline, and specific quality standards that must be met.

During a recent inspection, ABC Construction's quality control team identified numerous deficiencies in XYZ Electrical's work. These issues range from improper wiring and faulty connections to non-compliant installations that violate local building codes, resulting in significant project delays. This has created a ripple effect, impacted the work of other trades and is jeopardizing the project's overall completion date. In particular, the sheetrock installers have proceeded with their work in areas where electrical wiring is incomplete, forcing electricians to remove newly installed sheetrock to access and rectify their work.

The project manager for ABC Construction has called an urgent meeting with the XYZ Electrical project manager to discuss the situation. Both parties are eager to find a solution that minimizes the impact on the project, but they have differing perspectives on the root causes of the issues and the best way to move forward.

Time: 45 minutes

Team Assignments and Objectives:

Team 1 (ABC Construction):

- Represent the general contractor's interests.
- Analyze the subcontract to identify any clauses related to non-conforming work, delays, and potential remedies.
- Prepare a list of specific deficiencies and their impact on the project.
- Develop a strategy for addressing the issues with XYZ Electrical, focusing on ensuring timely completion and high-quality work.

Team 2 (XYZ Electrical):

- Represent the subcontractor's interests.
- Review the subcontract and identify any mitigating factors or potential defenses.
- Propose a plan to correct the identified deficiencies and mitigate further delays.
- Address concerns about the impact on the project schedule and other trades.

Team 3 (Mediators):

- Act as neutral mediators to facilitate a constructive discussion between the two parties.
- Identify the key points of disagreement and potential areas of compromise.
- Help the parties reach a mutually agreeable solution that addresses the non-conforming work, minimizes delays, and preserves the working relationship.

Instructions:

Prepare: Each team should thoroughly review the case scenario and relevant documents to understand their assigned role and objectives.

Meet and Discuss: The teams should meet separately to develop their strategies and arguments.

Negotiate: Teams 1 and 2 should then engage in a negotiation session, facilitated by Team 3 (mediators), to try and reach a resolution.

Present Outcomes: Each team should present a summary of their position, the key points of negotiation, and the agreed-upon solution (if any) to the class.

SUBCONTRACT AGREEMENT

This Subcontract Agreement ("Agreement") is made and entered into as of this [Date] day of [Month], [Year], by and between:

ABC Construction, a [State] company with its principal place of business at [Address], hereinafter referred to as "Contractor,"

and

XYZ Electrical, a [State] company with its principal place of business at [Address], hereinafter referred to as "Subcontractor."

WITNESSETH:

WHEREAS, Contractor has entered into a contract with [Owner Name] (the "Prime Contract") for the construction of [Project Name] located at [Project Address] (the "Project"); and

WHEREAS, Contractor desires to engage Subcontractor to perform certain electrical work on the Project, as more particularly described in Exhibit A (the "Scope of Work");

NOW, THEREFORE, in consideration of the mutual covenants and promises contained herein, the parties agree as follows:

SCOPE OF WORK

Subcontractor shall furnish all labor, materials, equipment, tools, supervision, and other items necessary to complete the Scope of Work in accordance with the plans, specifications, and other documents referenced in the Prime Contract (collectively, the "Contract Documents").

WARRANTY AND CORRECTION OF NONCONFORMING WORK

2.1 Warranty: Subcontractor warrants that all work performed under this Agreement will be free from defects in materials and workmanship and will conform to the requirements of the Contract Documents for a period of one (1) year from the date of Substantial Completion of the Project.

2.2 Notice of Nonconformance: If Contractor discovers any work that does not conform to the requirements of the Contract Documents ("Nonconforming Work"), Contractor shall give Subcontractor prompt written notice describing the Nonconforming Work in reasonable detail.

2.3 Timely Correction: Within [Number] days after receipt of such notice, Subcontractor shall, at its sole cost and expense, promptly correct the Nonconforming Work to the satisfaction of Contractor and in accordance with the Contract Documents.

DEFAULT

3.1 Grounds for Default: Contractor may terminate this Agreement for default if Subcontractor: Fails to make progress in the Work so as to endanger performance of this Agreement in accordance with its terms, and does not cure such failure within ten (10) days after receipt of written notice from Contractor; or

b) Fails to perform any of the other provisions of this Agreement, including, but not limited to, failing to correct Nonconforming Work as required by Section 2.3, and does not cure such failure within ten (10) days after receipt of written notice from Contractor; or

c) Fails to complete the Scope of Work by the time specified in this Agreement, unless the delay arises from causes beyond the control and without the fault or negligence of Subcontractor.

3.2 Contractor's Rights Upon Termination: In the event of termination for default, Contractor may procure, upon such terms and in such manner as Contractor may deem appropriate, labor, materials, and equipment similar to those so terminated, and Subcontractor shall be liable to Contractor for any excess costs for such similar labor, materials, and equipment.

3.3 Survival of Obligations: Termination of this Agreement for default shall not relieve Subcontractor of any liability to Contractor for damages sustained by Contractor by reason of any default by Subcontractor, and Subcontractor shall be liable to Contractor for all costs and expenses, including reasonable attorneys' fees, incurred by Contractor in enforcing its rights under this Agreement.

Notice Letter

Subject: Notice of Nonconforming Work and Delay

This letter serves as formal notice of nonconforming work and resulting delays on the [Project Name] project located at [Project Address].

During our inspection on [Date], we identified the following deficiencies in your work:

[List specific instances of nonconforming work, referencing relevant contract documents or standards]

These deficiencies do not meet the quality standards specified in our subcontract agreement dated [Date]. As a result, your nonconforming work is causing delays to the following trades:

[List affected trades and the specific impact of the delays]

We request that you take immediate corrective action to bring your work into full compliance with the contract specifications. Please provide us with a detailed plan outlining the corrective actions you will take and the expected completion date by [Deadline for Response].

Failure to take corrective action within the specified timeframe may result in the following consequences:

[List potential consequences, such as termination, back charges, or legal action]

We value our working relationship with XYZ Electrical and hope to resolve this issue amicably. Please contact us immediately to discuss this matter further.

ABC Construction reserves all rights and remedies in this matter.

Notes:

Case Study 4: Damage to Underground Utilities Due to Subcontractor Negligence

ABC Construction, a general contractor known for its substation projects, is expanding an energized brownfield substation. To expedite the project due to a tight schedule, ABC subcontracted PileCo, a smaller firm with limited substation experience, for pile driving. PileCo was chosen primarily due to their competitive bid and their inclusion on the Owner's Preferred Vendor List.

Before work began, PileCo received comprehensive plans, specifications, and a detailed site walk-through. They also participated in a safety meeting emphasizing the hazards of working in energized environments. However, the specific locations of existing underground utilities were not explicitly discussed during this meeting, nor were they clearly marked on the provided plans.

During pile driving operations, PileCo's crew, comprised of workers with minimal experience in energized substations, inadvertently struck an unmarked, energized underground utility line. This resulted in a major power outage, severely impacting the construction site and the surrounding community, including hospitals, traffic signals, and businesses.

ABC Construction immediately halted PileCo's work, activated their emergency response plan, and promptly notified the Owner. Recognizing the severity of the situation, the Owner issued a STOP WORK order for the entire project while the full extent of the damages was assessed.

Time: 45 minutes

Key Documents:

- Subcontract Agreement
- Engineer's Notes
- Project Manager's Notes
- Notice Letter to PileCo

Team Assignments and Objectives:

Team 1: ABC Construction

Role: You are the Project Manager for ABC Construction, the general contractor on the substation expansion project. You have been tasked by upper management to conduct a comprehensive review of the incident involving PileCo, the subcontractor responsible for pile driving. Your primary objectives are to:

- Protect ABC Construction's Interests: Thoroughly analyze the situation to determine the extent of ABC's liability and identify any potential avenues for mitigating financial losses and project delays.
- Minimize Losses and Delays: Develop a strategic plan to address the immediate aftermath of the incident, including repairs, project rescheduling, and communication with stakeholders.
- Maintain Owner Relationship: Prioritize open and transparent communication with the Owner to address their concerns, maintain trust, and collaborate on finding solutions to minimize disruptions to the project timeline and budget.

- Hold PileCo Accountable: Assess PileCo's contractual obligations and determine the appropriate course of action to hold them responsible for their negligence, whether through negotiation, back charges, insurance claims, or potential legal recourse.

Your leadership expects a detailed report outlining your findings, recommendations, and a clear plan of action to resolve this issue while safeguarding ABC Construction's reputation and financial well-being.

Team 2: PileCo

Role: You are the subcontractor, PileCo. Your goal is to minimize your liability, avoid significant financial losses, and maintain your reputation in the industry.

Objectives:

- Review the subcontract agreement and identify any potential defenses or mitigating factors, such as ambiguities in the contract or insufficient information provided by ABC Construction.
- Gather evidence to support your position, highlighting any factors that may have contributed to the incident, such as unclear markings of underground utilities or inadequate safety instructions.
- Prepare arguments to counter ABC Construction's claims of negligence and negotiate a settlement that limits your financial exposure.
- Develop a plan to demonstrate your commitment to safety and prevent similar incidents in the future.

Team 3: Neutral Observer

Role: You are an independent consultant hired to assess the situation and provide an unbiased evaluation of the dispute between ABC Construction and PileCo.

Objectives:

- Review all relevant documents, including the subcontract agreement, correspondence between the parties, and any available evidence related to the incident.
- Conduct interviews with representatives from ABC Construction and PileCo to gather their perspectives and understand their positions.
- Analyze the facts and circumstances of the case, considering contractual obligations, industry standards, and relevant legal principles.
- Identify the strengths and weaknesses of each party's arguments and assess their potential liability.
- Propose a fair and reasonable resolution to the dispute, taking into account the interests of both parties and the need to mitigate further damages and delays.
- Recommend preventive measures to avoid similar incidents in future projects.

CONSTRUCTION SUBCONTRACT AGREEMENT

This Subcontract Agreement ("Agreement") is made and entered into this [Date] by and between:

ABC Construction ("Contractor"), a [State] corporation with its principal place of business at [Address], and

PileCo ("Subcontractor"), a [State] corporation with its principal place of business at [Address].

WITNESSETH:

WHEREAS, Contractor has entered into a contract with [Owner Name] ("Owner") dated [Date of Prime Contract] ("Prime Contract") for the construction of the [Project Name] ("Project"); and

WHEREAS, Contractor desires to subcontract to Subcontractor a portion of the Work as described herein; and

WHEREAS, Subcontractor is ready, willing, and able to perform such Work.

NOW, THEREFORE, in consideration of the mutual covenants and promises contained herein, the parties agree as follows:

1. DEFINITIONS

1.1 Contract Documents: The Contract Documents shall consist of this Agreement, the Prime Contract (including all plans, specifications, drawings, addenda, and other documents incorporated therein), and any change orders or modifications issued in accordance with this Agreement.

1.2 Work: The Work shall consist of all labor, materials, equipment, and services necessary to complete the pile driving operations as described in the Contract Documents.

2. SCOPE OF WORK

2.1 Subcontractor shall furnish all labor, materials, equipment, supervision, and other services necessary to perform the Work in accordance with the Contract Documents.

2.2 Subcontractor shall complete the Work in accordance with the schedule set forth in the Contract Documents, as modified from time to time in accordance with this Agreement.

3. INCORPORATION OF PRIME CONTRACT

3.1 The Prime Contract is hereby incorporated into this Agreement by reference and made a part hereof as if fully set forth herein.

3.2 Subcontractor shall be bound to Contractor by the terms of the Prime Contract and shall assume toward Contractor all the obligations and responsibilities that Contractor, by the Prime Contract, assumes toward Owner.

4. COMPENSATION

4.1 Contractor shall pay Subcontractor for the Work the sum of [Amount] in accordance with the payment schedule set forth in the Contract Documents.

4.2 Payment shall be made upon submission of invoices by Subcontractor and approval by Contractor in accordance with the procedures set forth in the Contract Documents.

5. SAFETY REQUIREMENTS

5.1 Subcontractor shall comply with all applicable federal, state, and local safety laws, regulations, and ordinances, as well as any additional safety requirements set forth in the Contract Documents.

5.2 Subcontractor shall be responsible for the safety of its employees, agents, and subcontractors, and shall take all reasonable precautions to prevent accidents and injuries.

5.3 Subcontractor shall participate in all safety meetings and training sessions conducted by Contractor.

5.4 Subcontractor shall immediately report any accidents, injuries, or safety hazards to Contractor.

6. NOTICE REQUIREMENTS

6.1 Any notice required or permitted under this Agreement shall be in writing and shall be deemed to have been duly given when delivered personally, by confirmed email, or by certified or registered mail, postage prepaid, return receipt requested, to the party to whom such notice is directed at the address set forth in this Agreement.

7. RIGHT TO STOP WORK AND TERMINATE

7.1 Contractor reserves the right to stop all or any part of the Work if Subcontractor fails to comply with the safety requirements set forth in this Agreement or the Contract Documents, or if Subcontractor's performance of the Work creates an imminent danger to life or property.

7.2 If Contractor stops the Work in accordance with this Section, Subcontractor shall not be entitled to any additional compensation for any delays or increased costs resulting from such stoppage.

7.3 If Subcontractor fails to correct the safety violation or imminent danger within a reasonable time after receiving notice from Contractor, Contractor may terminate this Agreement for cause.

Notes Taken by Project Manager

- During a thorough review of the owner-provided drawings and plans, an engineer employed by ABC Construction discovered a 75-year-old drawing depicting the energized underground utility line. This drawing, dating back approximately 75 years, featured hand-drawn markings and annotations indicating the presence and location of the line. Notably, no other drawings or documents within the provided set referenced or depicted the existence of this line.
- Following the incident, I spoke with PileCo's Project Manager over the phone. He stated that they were unaware of any underground utilities at the site and confirmed that they had not contacted to request utility line locates prior to commencing pile driving activities.

Notice Letter to PileCo

SUBJECT: NOTICE OF NON-CONFORMING WORK AND DAMAGES

This letter serves as formal notice of non-conforming work and resulting damages on the [Project Name] project located at [Project Address].

On [Date], your crew, while performing pile driving operations, damaged an energized underground utility line. This resulted in a power outage that caused a complete shutdown of the construction site, halting all work.

This incident constitutes a breach of your contractual obligations, specifically the following:

Failure to exercise reasonable care in identifying and avoiding underground utilities, as per Section [Section Number] of the subcontract agreement.

Causing delays and disruptions to the project schedule, impacting other trades and incurring additional costs for ABC Construction.

As a result of your negligence, we are hereby notifying you that:

- Work Stoppage: You are instructed to cease all work on the project immediately until further notice.
- Investigation: We are conducting a thorough investigation to assess the full extent of the damages caused by this incident.
- Backcharges: You will be held responsible for all costs and damages incurred by ABC Construction due to the power outage and work stoppage, including but not limited to:
    - Lost productivity and labor costs
    - Equipment rental fees
    - Increased material costs due to delays
    - Potential liquidated damages for project delays

Corrective Action: Upon completion of the investigation and repair of the damaged utility line, you will be required to submit a detailed site safety plan to prevent similar incidents in the future.

We will notify you when you can resume work on the project, pending the owner's approval and the implementation of your site safety plan.

We expect your full cooperation in resolving this matter promptly and amicably. Failure to do so may result in further legal action.

ABC Construction reserves and rights and remedies in this matter.

Discussion Questions

1. **To what extent is each party (ABC, PileCo, and potentially the Owner) liable for the incident and resulting damages?**

____

____

____

____

2. **What are the strongest arguments for and against each party's liability?**

3. **How might the existence of the 75-year-old drawing impact the assignment of liability?**

4. **Did PileCo breach its contractual obligations by failing to identify and avoid underground utilities?**

5. **Are there any ambiguities or gaps in the subcontract agreement that could be used to strengthen either party's position?**

6. **What risk mitigation strategies could ABC Construction have implemented to minimize the likelihood of such an incident?**

7. What are the most viable options for ABC Construction to recover damages from PileCo – negotiation, back charges, insurance claims, or litigation?

8. Preventive Measures: Based on your analysis, what specific recommendations would you make to prevent similar incidents in future projects?

Conclusion

In conclusion, this comprehensive study guide has equipped you with a solid foundation in contract law and its practical application. We have covered the fundamentals of contract language, risk reduction strategies, the intricacies of notices, waivers, and change orders, best practices for documentation, navigating subcontractor claims and disputes, and effective communication and relationship management. Additionally, we have delved into the complexities of preparing, drafting, and defending claims, providing you with the knowledge and tools to navigate these challenging situations.

By completing the case studies, you have gained valuable hands-on experience in analyzing real-world scenarios, applying contract principles, and developing effective strategies for dispute resolution. This knowledge will undoubtedly enhance your ability to perform your job more effectively, minimizing risks, preventing disputes, and ensuring successful project outcomes.

As you continue your career in the construction industry, remember that contract law is constantly evolving. Stay abreast of changes in legislation, regulations, and industry standards to ensure your knowledge remains current and relevant. Engage legal counsel when faced with complex or contentious issues, and always keep your leadership informed of any potential risks or disputes. By embracing lifelong learning and proactive risk management, you can navigate the complexities of construction contracts with confidence and achieve continued success in your professional endeavors.

Let's Stay in Touch!

Dear Reader,

I hope you enjoyed the lessons outlined in this workbook and that the stories and insights shared within have resonated with you. I invite you to continue our dialogue. If you have questions, feedback, or would like to discuss potential collaborations or workshops, please contact me at dondi.day@emeraldislepublishing.com. I am also available for speaking engagements and book signings.

For traditional mail correspondence, please use the following address:

P.O. Box 5041
Emerald Isle, NC 28594-5041

If you enjoyed the book, leaving a review on Goodreads.com or Amazon.com would help others discover it. Thank you for your support!

I look forward to hearing from you, and I hope our paths cross again soon.

Sincerely,

Dr. Dondi M. Day

PS. You can find me on LinkedIn @ https://www.linkedin.com/in/dondimday/ or on the book of faces @ https://www.facebook.com/profile.php?id=61560913719838

Notes:

www.ingramcontent.com/pod-product-compliance
Ingram Content Group UK Ltd.
Pitfield, Milton Keynes, MK11 3LW, UK
UKHW061829190726
13853UKWH00009B/2526